Science Fair Projects for Elementary Schools

Step by Step

Patricia Hachten Wee

The Scarecrow Press, Inc.
Lanham, Maryland, & London
1998

SCARECROW PRESS, INC.

Published in the United States of America
by Scarecrow Press, Inc.
4720 Boston Way
Lanham, Maryland 20706

4 Pleydell Gardens, Folkestone
Kent CT20 2DN, England

Copyright © 1998 by Patricia Hachten Wee

British Library Cataloguing in Publication Information Available

Library of Congress Cataloging-in-Publication Data

Wee, Patricia Hachten, 1948-
    Science fair projects for elementary schools : step by step / Patricia Hachten Wee.
        p.   cm.
    Includes bibliographical references and index.
    ISBN 0-8108-3543-6 (alk. paper)
    1. Science projects--Handbooks, manuals, etc. 2. Science--Exhibitions--Handbooks, manuals, etc. I. Title.
    Q182.3.W44   1998
    507.8--dc21   98-30432
                                                        CIP

☉™ The paper used in this publication meets the minimum requirements of American National Standard for Information Sciences—Permanence of Paper for Printed Library Materials, ANSI Z39.48–1984.
Manufactured in the United States of America.

for my husband, Robert,
my son, Adam,
and my grandchildren, Michael and Erin

Contents

Acknowledgments

Many thanks to the media center staff, Deb, Candy, Chris, and Peggy, and computer wizard, Dave Cherry. I wish to express very special gratitude to Karen Leonhard for her steadfast support and constant help. As always, I could never have completed this book without my dear husband's never-failing encouragement.

PART 1

HOW TO USE THIS BOOK

CHAPTER 1

The Importance of Science Fair Projects

One of the greatest joys of science is discovery. When we give children a chance to discover something on their own, we provide not only an exciting scientific experience but also a real life experience.

Completing a science fair project allows the child to actually *be* a scientist. While we regularly afford children an abundance of opportunities to relish the natural world and to sample science, we rarely give them the chance to *experience* science — with its requirements of hard work, tenacity, and creativity.

Working through a science fair project to its completion provides a child with life skills that will extend beyond the science classroom and beyond school itself. *Science for All Americans*, the landmark collaboration of several hundred scientists, mathematicians, engineers, physicians, philosophers, historians, and educators, encourages us to "emphasize the exploration of questions . . . and critical thought" [1] in the education of our young people. Science teachers, librarians, and parents "should help students acquire both scientific knowledge of the world and scientific habits of mind." [2] Further, science education is in a particularly strong position to foster three highly desirable human attitudes and values—curiosity, openness to new ideas, and informed skepticism. [3]

Benchmarks for Science Literacy, the companion report to *Science for All Americans*, utilizes the comprehensive research of professional scientists and educators to describe a common core of learning that contributes to the science literacy of all students. It specifies how students should progress toward science literacy and recommends what students should know and be able to do by the time they reach certain grade levels. Among the recommendations or "benchmarks" given are:

By the end of second grade, students should
- raise questions about the world around them and be willing to seek answers to some of them by making careful observations and trying things out.[4]
- know that when a science investigation is done the way it was done before, we expect to get a very similar result.[5]
- realize that science investigations generally work out the same way in different places.[6]
- understand that people can often learn about things around them just by observing those things carefully, but sometimes they can learn more by doing something to the things and noting what happens.[7]
- be familiar with tools such as thermometers, magnifiers, rulers, or balances, which can often give more information about things than can be obtained by just observing without their help.[8]
- be able to describe things as accurately as possible because it enables people to compare their observations with those of others.[9]
- know that simple graphs can help to tell about observations.[10]

By the end of fifth grade, students should
- keep records of their investigations and observations and not change records later.[11]
- offer reasons for their findings and consider reasons suggested by others.[12]
- understand that scientific investigations may take many different forms, including observing, collecting specimens for analysis, and doing experiments.[13]
- realize that the results of scientific investigations are seldom exactly the same; but if the differences are large, it is important to try to figure out why. One reason for following directions carefully and for keeping records is to provide information on what might have caused the differences.[14]
- know that mathematical ideas can be represented concretely, graphically, and symbolically.[15]
- write instructions that others can follow in carrying out a procedure.[16]

Completing a science fair project provides the child with ample opportunities to achieve these benchmarks. Science fair project work stimulates critical thinking and builds problem-solving skills, teaches the child to seek answers and to make qualitative observations, and fosters logical reasoning.

While the use of the scientific method is essential to any research in science, there is no reason to concentrate on the terminology. A well-organized science fair project *is* the scientific method. Most children are naturally excited by science. As educators, librarians, and parents, we can foster this attitude by encouraging children to become involved in science fair project work.

We would be ignoring reality, however, if we failed to recognize that some children have experienced frustration and failure in attempting to complete a science fair project. Feelings of disappointment are exactly what this book is designed to prevent by providing:

1. a structured format for the project,
2. well-organized sample projects,
3. ready-made projects in many fields, and
4. a variety of project ideas suitable for students in grades 2 through 5, a list of children's books related to projects and science topics, and an annotated bibliography of additional sources.

Children frequently become confused when trying to organize an entire project. They can omit important steps, make huge leaps from one point to another, and be left without adequate time to complete tasks. The structure of this book and the child's friendly companion throughout, THE CURIOSITY BUG , will overcome these problems. Chapter 3 explains how librarians, teachers, and parents should use *The Student's Science Fair Project Handbook* to the best advantage.

Having CURIOSITY BUG'S complete science fair project shown throughout the student's section provides a comforting template for the child to follow. Many resource books give only sketchy outlines of real projects; few, if any, provide a sample project taken from the beginning to the completion. CURIOSITY BUG starts just where the student will have to begin, with the selection of an idea, and progresses through all the steps with the child. Every step is explained and shown by CURIOSITY BUG . When the child is asked to make a data table, for example, CURIOSITY BUG explains what a data table is, shows exactly how to make a data table, and shares *his* completed data table.

For a child's first science fair project there are ten age-appropriate *cookbook style* projects in many areas of science provided in Part 3, *Sample Projects and Project Ideas*. These sample projects are set up with all the instructions on exactly how to do each part of the project. The child follows each step of the experiment, compiles the actual data, fills in the data tables and graph templates, and designs the display. Frustration is essentially eliminated and the success of the completed project is virtually assured.

Following the sample projects in Part 3 are lists of ideas for a student's subsequent science fair project. The ideas are suitable for these grade levels, but can be modified for use with older children as well. The lists are organized into the same general fields as the sample projects:

- Projects with Plants,
- Projects with Animals and Insects,
- Projects in Chemistry,
- Projects on the Environment,
- Projects with Microscopes.

To enhance interest in science and science fair projects a list of current children's literature has been compiled by topic. Teachers, librarians, and parents can utilize these books to integrate science into other subject areas, disciplines, and assignments.

Part 4 provides detailed information on how to set up a science fair, including time schedules and various forms that may be used in organizing a science fair. Often the only reason that a school has for not holding a science fair is that no one has taken on the responsibility of organizing it. While the idea may seem daunting, the process can be quite manageable with the guidelines offered in Part 4.

The annotated bibliography provides a substantial listing of other resource books that are helpful in researching topic ideas, finding experimental procedures, and extending topics. Annotations include which ideas offered are suitable for science fair projects; the number of experiments, projects, or activities provided; the complexity of the items; the adequacy of safety guidelines; the presence of detailed instructions; the amount of adult supervision required; and the usefulness of background information. The ease of use of each publication may be indicated by the kind and number of features listed, such as a table of contents, list of suppliers, glossary, or index.

Notes

1. F. James Rutherford, *Science for All Americans, Project 2061* (New York: Oxford University Press, 1994), xvi.
2. Rutherford, *Science*, 203.
3. Rutherford, *Science*, 185.
4. American Association for the Advancement of Science, *Benchmarks for Science Literacy, Project 2061* (New York: Oxford University Press, 1993), 285.
5. AAAS, *Benchmarks*, 6.
6. AAAS, *Benchmarks*, 6.
7. AAAS, *Benchmarks*, 10.

8. AAAS, *Benchmarks*, 10.
9. AAAS, *Benchmarks*, 10.
10. AAAS, *Benchmarks*, 211.
11. AAAS, *Benchmarks*, 286.
12. AAAS, *Benchmarks*, 286.
13. AAAS, *Benchmarks*, 11.
14. AAAS, *Benchmarks*, 11.
15. AAAS, *Benchmarks*, 27.
16. AAAS, *Benchmarks*, 296.

CHAPTER 2

Getting Started

One of the hardest parts of a science fair project for all involved is finding an idea. A successful science fair project that is educationally sound must be based on actual data gathering. While collections, demonstrations, models, and reports are useful in other respects, they do not afford the child the opportunity to *be* a scientist.

Typically teachers, parents, and librarians struggle to suggest a variety of topics, while the student determinedly rejects all offered ideas. The easiest solution to this dilemma is to read through Part 2, *The Student's Science Fair Project Handbook*, together. This can be done at home with the parents selecting the time and duration or in the classroom with the teacher or as part of a library unit where the librarian will serve as the leader. Once the children become comfortable with CURIOSITY BUG'S progress through the example project, they will be receptive to assistance in selecting a project topic.

At this point it is advisable to read through the ideas found in Part 3, *Sample Projects and Project Ideas*. Allow the child some time to peruse the possibilities. For a first science fair project it may be easiest for everyone to select one of the sample projects in Part 3. These sample projects are completely described and each step is clearly explained. Sample projects are organized into the general fields of plants, animals and insects, chemistry, physical science, and the environment. Following these "cookbook" directions will provide the student with a highly structured excursion into the new world of science fair projects. Use of a sample project will ensure the child a successful educational experience that is virtually free of frustration; and, what may be more important at this stage, it will be *fun!*

As the child becomes more experienced with project work, the lists of other ideas in the chapters of Part 3 will be useful. Ideas for many science fair projects in the same general field follow the sample projects in each chapter of Part 3. Each idea has numbered references to the books listed in the bibliography. When the student finds a topic of interest, several publications that feature that specific area can be easily provided. This will enable the child to stay focused and will avoid unnecessary delay in moving along with the project.

Always help the student keep pace with the time schedules and complete each worksheet. Several time schedules are given in Appendix A.

CHAPTER 3

Instructions for Each Step of the Student's Science Fair Project Handbook

The usefulness of this book will be enhanced by the use of this chapter of instructions for the adults involved. Part 2, *The Student's Science Fair Project Handbook* , is organized into 16 steps. Parents and teachers should read this chapter and Part 2 completely before the child begins. Detailed instructions about how to use each step to the child's best advantage follow.

Step 1   A Science Fair Project
Step 2   Thinking about a Project
Step 3   Picking a Project

These three steps should be taken as a unit. They may be done over several days and will culminate in the selection of a science fair project idea. While adhering to a time schedule is always important, try not to rush the child's choice of an idea to pursue. Beginning these three steps midweek, working through them over the remainder of the week and into the weekend, and completing Worksheet 1 in Step 3 on Sunday afternoon is a reasonable time frame. This allows the child to seek the teacher's advice on Monday, if necessary, and provides an exciting beginning to the new week with the child knowing what his or her science fair project will be. To make a science fair project most educationally sound, the student needs to do some *real* science. This means that the child will actually gather data: measure something or count something. (Note that the word *data* has evolved to encompass the singular and the plural. Historically, *data* was plural, as in "data are collected;" and the singular was *datum*. Today, many publications accept data as either singular or plural. You may say "data are" or "data is.") There are occasions when a collection or a report can be worthwhile, but generally a science fair project must be of the data-gathering type. Most topics will lend themselves to several data-gathering projects. The example projects in *The Student's Science Fair Project Handbook* and the sample projects and ideas for projects in chapters 4 through 8 are all data-gathering projects. After reading through these chapters, you will be able to see other possibilities for developing data-gathering science fair projects. CURIOSITY BUG'S list of ideas in Steps 1 and 2 set an example for the types of projects needed. They are data-gathering in nature and center on topics familiar to children and within their reach. Nevertheless, probably nothing will assuredly prevent the inclusion of the occasional *wild* idea proffered by a precocious second grader, such as wanting to build a talking robot!

While the selection process is proceeding, parents should try to take the family's situation into account. If space in your home absolutely prohibits a project such as the light bulb comparison (CURIOSITY BUG'S second idea, page 31) because you do not have an unoccupied room to place continuously lighted lamps, try to steer your child away from that type of project. Instead, suggest one that can be completed with a minimum of space; for example, counting the number of seeds on dandelions. This project can be managed on the kitchen table and stored in plastic bags in a shoe box. If you live in the city without a yard, direct the discussion of topics away from counting weeds or insects and try to encourage projects dealing with house plants or chemistry. You will want to read through the ideas offered *before* the child chooses a project so that you will have had time to consider your individual circumstances.

As the child completes Steps 1 and 2, think ahead to what is required on Worksheet 1 in Step 3. If you have some clear ideas of what might be counted or measured, it will enable you to direct discussion adequately.

Step 4   **Planning Your Project**
Step 5   **Safety**

Before the student begins Step 4, the supervising adult should read over the safety information in Step 5. This will assist you in helping the student plan the project. One of the first things the child should list on Worksheet 2 is library research on the topic. Take advantage of the *Annotated Bibliography* at this point to find books that directly relate to the child's topic. Parents can arrange a visit to the public library soon after the completion of this worksheet and teachers will want to plan a library visit for the class. If you have access to the Internet, you can use the resources there as well. School librarians will be better able to assist if they have advance notice of the project topics for the class.

Help the child think of all the steps to be taken for the project's completion. A well-planned experimental procedure will prevent many problems. Of course, it is virtually impossible to think of everything; so do not be too surprised if some obstacles are encountered. The suggested time schedules should allow adequate time to overcome a few minor glitches.

Carefully discuss the safety guidelines in Step 5 with the child. While the sample projects provided in this book have rigorous safety precautions, the experimental procedures for other projects developed from the lists of ideas will need to be conscientiously scrutinized for the safety precautions given in Step 5. Most projects for this age group will be covered by the safety points in the step. If you have concerns, though, have the procedure screened by someone knowledgeable in the field. Note that all sample projects are marked with the following safety warnings where needed:

This is the time to analyze the actual space and equipment requirements of the project. For parents, this means considering:

- where and when your child will work on the project,
- where the supplies will be kept,
- how to ensure that younger siblings will not have access to the project,
- what to do with a portion of an experiment that has only been partially completed by bedtime,
- where things can be hidden away if company comes,
- and how to be sure the family pet will not eat the project.

Most students will work on their science fair projects at home. A few, however, may require some space in the classroom. The space limitations of the classroom will determine if any or all projects can be set up at school. The teacher will have to weigh the benefits of having projects in the classroom against the disadvantages. With projects in the school room, the teacher will be able to monitor the student's progress in a more detailed manner and to offer guidance and assistance readily. This option will, however, require much more of the teacher's time. The teacher will become an all-day resource person and problem-solver. It will also create certain other problems, such as weekend and vacation care of plants and animals. The teacher should resolve this dilemma before introducing the science fair project assignment.

Step 6   Planning to Gather Data
Step 7   Getting Ready

Children often make big jumps between steps and will omit important parts of the experiment. You will need to help the student with the details of the experiment. Step 6 explains how to gather data and how to record the data in tables. Step 7 introduces the concept of controlled experimentation. The plans made on Worksheet 2 are refined in these steps. Definite procedures for counting or measuring are made and the experimental control is added.

It is important for the supervising adult to determine if the child has been introduced to the metric system (meters, liters, and grams). As a general rule, measurements for science fair projects must be made in metric units. However, if the student has not yet been taught this system, the English system (inches/feet, ounces/gallons, ounces/pounds) may be used.

Brenda Walpole's *Measure Up with Science* series (bibliography nos. 60 - 63) is an excellent source for metric system units; for measuring area, volume, capacity, weight, mass, and temperature; and for using estimation, triangulation, and scale drawings. Developing skill in measurements is one additional benefit gained from science fair projects. The teacher or parents should ensure that the child plans to measure the "right" thing and plans to use the correct method and unit.

Worksheet 3 provides a data table to be modified for the student's own science fair project. Use of a computer for making data tables is also mentioned. If the child has access to a computer this is an opportune time to introduce the educational uses of software.

In Step 7, Getting Ready, you will need to help the child with other details of the experiment. A science fair project must be based upon a controlled experiment. CURIOSITY BUG explains the concept to the child as "only one thing is changed in the experiment. Sometimes it means only counting things in one special place or measuring things after a certain amount of time." In projects where different plants or other organisms are treated in different ways, there must be a control group. No changes or differences in the environment are made to this set of organisms:

- the control plants are *not* given fertilizer,
- the control insects are *not* fed the special food.

The control group provides the standard to which the data from the experimental group can be compared.

It is likely that you will not catch all the possible pitfalls or problems that may arise during a project. Do not be overly concerned about this since it is a part of "real" science and all scientists encounter obstacles. Overcoming problems is an important part of science. The student will learn a great deal from fixing problems and from overcoming obstacles during the completion of the science fair project.

Worksheet 4 provides three templates for making the child's project a controlled experiment. One of the three choices should "fit" most projects. You will be able to help modify the choices if needed.

Step 8   Your Experimental Notebook

The student will need to keep track of what is supposed to be done, what has been completed, and what has been learned. A science fair project requires an experimental notebook. For this age group a three-ring binder is suggested.

The checklist in Step 8 presents the essential parts of an experimental notebook. The worksheets you reproduce from *The Student's Science Fair Project Handbook* and provide to the student will be placed in the experimental notebook. Each worksheet is numbered and has the drawing opposite to remind the child to place the page in the experimental notebook.

Put this page in your Experimental Notebook

The completed worksheets provide all the basic elements for the display. It would be wise to photocopy the completed worksheets to keep at home or at school in case the originals are misplaced.

Step 9   Experimenting

As the student begins reading about the project topic and getting ready to begin experimenting, be sure to encourage daily record keeping in the experimental notebook. It is important for the child to write short descriptions of what has been found in the books. An example of what should be recorded is found in Step 10, page 43. You will want to help the student keep a written log of the steps taken in finding the materials, designing the procedure, and any other planning activities. Each entry should be dated.

A schedule should be made to show when the child will work on the project. Be sure that you have thought about convenient times in your own schedule. The number of days per week and the number of hours per day will depend largely upon the project itself. Some projects will require much more time than others. If you can think about this *before* the time to make a schedule arrives, it may prevent some confusion. While the science fair project must be the student's own work, parents and teachers will need to assist.

Be certain to keep a rein on your desire to make the project perfect. No one expects the work of children of this age to be without some mistakes. You will, no doubt, become quite involved in the planning and design of the project; but, please, remember that this is the *child's* chance to be a scientist, not yours. Be a cheerleader, a facilitator, and a helper. Help the child stick to the schedule, but know when everyone needs a break.

This is also the time to decide if you will be able to help with photographing essential steps or parts of the project. Photographs can enhance a science fair project, but they are not essential. If you are going to take pictures, do it early enough so there is not a rush to get them developed. Photographs that might be used on the display would need to be in hand during the planning of that part of the project.

In Step 9 it is suggested that copies of data tables be made. This will depend upon the type of data to be collected. You will need to help the child make this determination. It is acceptable to photocopy blank data tables.

Step 10   Your Report

This step encourages the student to read about the project topic and provides an example of how to record notes. Each page of notes should be included in the experimental notebook. Help the child choose books that are both interesting and informative. Nonfiction books and encyclopedias will provide the most information. Some of the references in the *Annotated Bibliography* may be suitable. In the sample projects, specific references from the *Annotated Bibliography* have been noted in the section entitled "Books to read about this project." As the child reads information related to the project and takes notes, spend some time discussing the material. You will want to explain how certain facts or concepts are involved in the child's experiment.

CURIOSITY BUG explains scientific names in this step. It is not absolutely necessary to include the scientific names of the plants or animals involved in the project, but it is a chance to enlarge the child's understanding of science. No one will ask the student to pronounce the scientific name of an organism. Use of the common name throughout the remainder of the report is perfectly acceptable. If there is an oral presentation, the child will not be expected to say the scientific name.

Parts of the report can be written during "off" times of the project experimentation. If the student must wait a week between counting weeds in the yard or two weeks for plants to germinate, suggest that this time should be used to copy the notes they have taken into final form. This is also a good time to help the child design and construct an attractive cover for the report.

Step 11   The Experimental Method

Often students, teachers, and parents become caught up in the application of the scientific method to science fair projects. The scientific method *is* an important process; but what is truly significant is the "doing" of the process! It matters very little what one calls each stage of the scientific method; but it matters a great deal how one performs that step. The names of the parts of the experimental method should be used as headings on the display:

- Purpose
- Procedure
- Experiment
- Observations
- Conclusion

The student will become comfortable with these names by the completion of the project. It is not necessary to drill the child about the names of the steps. Rather, encourage the student to notice what has already been done that "qualifies" as part of the experimental method. In Step 11 CURIOSITY BUG explains this to the child in a table.

Be certain that you emphasize the importance of accurately recording the data observed. Sometimes a child (or a parent, for that matter) will have a preconceived idea of what the experiment should show or of what effects should be seen. One of the most important attitudes that can be developed during a science fair project is that of integrity. A scientist must always report exactly what happened—not what he or she hoped would happen. Please use this opportunity to foster this attitude.

Many times young researchers are disappointed if the project does not produce exciting results or if it does not show what they thought should or would happen. This is one of the realities of scientific research. Children should have the chance to learn early on that negative results are, in and of themselves, important.

Step 12   Understanding Your Data

This is the next stumbling block for most science fair projects. Students of all ages tend to either ignore the meaning of the data or tend to make large leaps toward the significance of the data.

CURIOSITY BUG presents *his* completed data tables to the child and then explains how to make sense of the data. Sometimes another table that shows the totals is helpful, as in the example project. Discuss how this table enables the child to see the information in a different light and how it facilitates writing a brief discussion of the observations. In most cases, it is essential that the data be shown in tables, in graphs (explained in Step 13), and in a short paragraph. Discuss how the written material clarifies what is presented in the tables. The evaluator, the teacher, or the judge of the project will understand the data better if all three methods are used. Moreover, the child will understand the meaning of the data more completely.

A set of leading questions provides a means by which you and the student can determine what the data means:

- Would a table with the total number help me?
- Did one thing happen the most?
- Did one thing happen the least?
- Would the average number help me?
- Did one kind change more than the others?
- Did all the things change in the same way?

These guidelines may not "fit" all science fair projects, but they should give you some direction in approaching how to help the child understand the meaning of the data.

Step 13   Making Graphs

Most children will have been taught how to make graphs in school during second or third grade. However, CURIOSITY BUG'S step-by-step explanation may clarify the methods. Work with the student through each step in making a practice graph.

Even much older pupils sometimes have difficulty determining a scale for each axis of a graph. All the graphs in a project should have the same scale for ease of comparison. In the example project, CURIOSITY BUG chose 1 square to represent 1 weed. Be sure to look at all the child's data before deciding on a scale to use.

All the mistakes should be made on the practice graph. You may want to encourage the child to make a practice graph for each final graph to be used. This may seem like a great deal of effort, but it will definitely make the end results much more satisfactory. Final copies of the graphs should be made with erasable ink to prevent smudging.

Avoid buying graph paper with too small a grid. Graph paper with one-centimeter squares or one-half-inch squares will be the easiest for children of this age to use. Graph paper with white margins on all sides is preferable. The margins may provide enough space to print the title of the graph.

Determination of which type of graph to make depends upon the data to be graphed. Most projects for this age group will generate data that can be adequately displayed by a bar graph. This is the type of graph explained in detail in Step 13. The child can color the bars with colored pencils or you can help cut strips of colored construction paper to paste into each bar. An alternate method is to cut the colored tape used in label makers to fit the bars. Avoid having the student use markers. These are difficult to use neatly and often make the graph look untidy.

Pictographs are a kind of bar graph in which the bars are replaced by pictures related to the data. You may design a pictograph by drawing the picture to the size of the bar required as shown below.

The example given in Step 13 uses a small picture of a light bulb to represent a certain number of hours the bulb burned or it could show a certain number of bulbs.

If the child has access to a computer and graphing software, you can help explain its use. Avoid doing the graphing for the student. One of the most important parts of a science fair project is learning how to do all the activities involved. Teach the child how to make a graph, and the child will have a new skill to be used in other contexts. Some software programs make very complicated graphs that may interfere with the understanding of the data.

Step 14   Your Conclusion

The conclusion of a science fair project is generally much shorter than children want it to be. It is the "answer" to the question asked in the purpose. It should be no longer that three sentences. Children tend to want to tell everything they have learned over the course of the project, but the conclusion is not the place for this.

Ask the child to tell you the answer to the idea selected at the bottom of Worksheet 1 (page 30). The question in the example project is "How many kinds of weeds grow in my yard?" The answer is "Five different kinds of weeds." This answer is the conclusion. It should be amplified to tell the different types of weeds and a small amount of other information.

If there is pertinent material that the child feels must be explained, do it in the observations section. There is no generally accepted limit to the amount of material that can be discussed in the written portion of the observations. CURIOSITY BUG could have listed the number of each type of weed found instead of only the number of the most common and least common weeds.

Step 15   Your Display

Constructing the display for the science fair project is one of the most enjoyable and creative parts. While this step is presented toward the end, it should be read much earlier. A good time to skip ahead to planning the display is during one of the waiting periods; while the student is waiting for the plants to germinate or for the crystals to grow.

The purpose of the backboard is to give sturdy support to the display. All the child's hard work on the project can be shown to a disadvantage if the display sags or falls over. The backboard of the display is something that parents can construct for the child. You should enlist the student's help with the building of the supporting backboard, but no one expects the child to do this part alone.

What kind of backboards you select depends upon your building skills, your time schedule, and your budget. Several companies manufacture ready-to-use display boards of heavy, laminated cardboard. Addresses for these companies are in *Appendix B*. There are many materials that can be used for the backboard, including cardboard, plywood, paneling, foam board, pegboard, foam insulation sheets, and others. Construction of the backboard can be elaborate or simple:

- a large sturdy cardboard box with the top, bottom, and one side cut away,
- two pieces of scrap plywood that are hinged together with duct tape,
- one piece of scrap paneling with an easel-type back support,
- a three-sided construction covered with fabric or wallpaper,
- or a hinged frame.

The title of the project and the headings for each section of the experimental method (Purpose, Procedure, Observations, Conclusion) can be made in a variety of ways. The words can be stenciled onto paper and mounted onto construction paper or poster board. They can be printed from a computer or spelled out with stick-on letters purchased at office supply stores. Some schools and churches have letter cutters or letter punches that you may be able to use. It is best to construct each heading and the title separately as individual pieces to avoid time-consuming mistakes. Avoid doing any lettering directly onto the backboard or its covering. Neatness is all-important in making the display.

You will want to help the child decide on the color scheme for the project that can be used for the backboard, the headings and title, and the report cover. If you choose to use a table cover, it is advisable to color coordinate it as well. Encourage everyone in the family to offer ideas. Grandparents and younger brothers and sisters often display great creativity and finally have the chance to get involved in the science fair project. Do not succumb to the temptation to completely take over this process, though. Always remember that it is the *child's* science fair project!

Be sure to check with the regulations limiting the kinds of items that can be displayed in your particular science fair. For safety reasons, some fairs have forbidden the use of plants, soil, insect mounts, chemicals, and other materials. Ask for a set of guidelines as soon as the child has decided to participate in the science fair.

Some items that can be displayed with the project are:

- photographs,
- photograph albums,
- examples of the organisms
  (Note: Your science fair may not allow live plants or animals.
  If this is the case, you may encourage the child to use a toy or
  stuffed animal or plastic plants),
- drawings,
- models,
- mounted specimens,

- samples that have been collected,
- parts of the experiment,
- representations of steps taken in the Procedure,
- measuring devices, or
- equipment.

The last two parts of the display are the experimental notebook and the report. The former does *not* have to be copied into a perfectly neat final form. No changes need be made in its content. Mistakes, spills, wrinkles are all acceptable. It is advisable, though, for the front of the notebook to be clean. You may want to help the child move all the pages into a new binder. The report, however, should be neat and should have an attractive cover.

Step 16   The Science Fair

You and the child will receive specific information about your science fair from the school. Mark the calendar with these important dates and times:

- set up of the display,
- judging (if your science fair will have judges),
- open house for the public,
- and dismantling of the display.

Step 16 provides a checklist for items to take along to the set up. You will, no doubt, think of other things that should be in your "emergency" bag. Add to the list anything that might be needed to repair damage done during transport of the backboards, such as extra hinging material, extra covering materials, extra construction paper, etc. If your child's display will require electricity, be sure to take your own power strip. You may arrive at the fair site and find only one outlet for four or five projects. Pack some additional poster board pieces or construction paper in case some of the headings or other material that has been mounted comes loose or is torn.

It is wise to listen to the weather report for predictions of rain or snow. If inclement weather is possible on the day of set up, cover the backboards with plastic garbage bags. Nothing upsets a child more than to see all his or her hard work "ruined" by an accident in handling or by raindrops.

If your science fair has a judging session that includes having the child make an oral presentation to the judges, help the student rehearse at home. Generally the oral presentation is made at the project to only one or two teachers, community members, or high school or college students. Rarely does a child of this age have to speak to a large group of people.

Set up the backboards on the kitchen or dining room table that has been covered with something to protect its surface. Have all the props displayed and let the child tell you about the project. Several rehearsals will help to eliminate nervousness. Assure the student that the judges just want to know what the child has done. Ask a few friendly questions during this practice judging session so that the child will not be surprised if the judge asks a question or two. If siblings are to be present at the practice sessions, discuss proper behavior with them beforehand. Sometimes older brothers or sisters may be tempted to ask hard questions or otherwise torment the project presenter.

These practice sessions will also show the child that he or she really does know everything about the project. After all, the student has worked on it for weeks, has read about the topic, and has analyzed the data. Who will know the project better than the child?

PART 2

THE STUDENT'S SCIENCE FAIR PROJECT HANDBOOK

THE STUDENT'S SCIENCE FAIR PROJECT HANDBOOK

- Step 1   A Science Fair Project
- Step 2   Thinking about a Project
- Step 3   Picking a Project

    Worksheet 1: Picking Your Project

- Step 4   Planning Your Project

    Worksheet 2: Planning Your Project

- Step 5   Safety
- Step 6   Planning to Gather Your Data

    Worksheet 3: Planning to Gather Your Data

- Step 7   Getting Ready

    Worksheet 4: Getting Ready

- Step 8   Your Experimental Notebook
- Step 9   Experimenting
- Step 10   Your Report
- Step 11   The Experimental Method
- Step 12   Understanding Your Data

    Worksheet 5: Understanding Your Data

- Step 13   Making Graphs
- Step 14   Your Conclusion

    Worksheet 6: Your Conclusion

- Step 15   Your Display
- Step 16   The Science Fair

STEP 1
A SCIENCE FAIR PROJECT

Hi! I'm Curiosity Bug.
I'm curious about the world
   just like you are.
A Science Fair Project is a fun
   way for you to find out
   something about the world
   for yourself.
Your parents, your teacher, and I
   will help you, but this is
   YOUR chance to be a real
   scientist!

A scientist wonders why something is the way it is.
   Are cats "right-handed"?
   How many seeds are on dandelions?
   Do some plants grow better with electricity?
   How many different kinds of insects can I catch in my yard?
There are lots of things you wonder about. One of them could be a Science
   Fair Project for you.
I'll help you with your project step by step on the pages that follow.

STEP 2
THINKING ABOUT A PROJECT

I want to help you find a project that will be fun for you to do.
What are some things in nature or at home that you wonder about?
Besides the questions on page 27, I wonder about:

How many kinds of weeds grow in my yard?

How long does a light bulb last?

How fast do plastic bags break down?

Do plants grow taller with fertilizer?

Make a list of 3 things you want to know about:

1._____

2._____

3._____

STEP 3
PICKING A PROJECT

You wrote some ideas on page 28.
Do you remember some of my ideas?
They all had something that you can
count or measure. Scientists call
this "DATA GATHERING."
A Science Fair Project is most fun if
you can count or measure
something.

Let's go back to my ideas and see what we could count or measure:

How many kinds of weeds grow in my yard?
COUNT THE NUMBER OF DIFFERENT KINDS OF WEEDS.

How long does a light bulb last?
COUNT THE NUMBER OF DAYS UNTIL THE LIGHT BULB BURNS
OUT.

How fast do plastic bags break down?
COUNT THE NUMBER OF DAYS UNTIL THE PLASTIC BAG
HAS HOLES IN IT.

Do plants grow taller with fertilizer?
MEASURE HOW TALL THE PLANTS GROW.

Let's see what you could count or measure with the ideas you listed on
page 28.

WORKSHEET 1
PICKING YOUR PROJECT

WHAT CAN YOU COUNT OR MEASURE WITH YOUR IDEAS?

Look back on page 28 to remember what you wrote
and
write below what you can count or measure for your ideas.
Follow the examples I gave on what I could count or measure for my
ideas.

1. For my idea # 1, I can count (or measure) _____

_____

_____

2. For my idea #2, I can count (or measure) _____

_____

_____

3. For my idea #3, I can count (or measure) _____

_____

_____

Which idea do you like best? Ask your parents or your teacher if they agree
with you, then write the idea you chose on the lines below.

My idea for my Science Fair Project: _____

_____

STEP 4
PLANNING YOUR PROJECT

Now you know what your Science
Fair Project will be.
I think you picked a very good idea!
What do you do next?
You must plan what you will do to
find out what you want to know.
What will you need to do to count or
measure?

Let's go back to two of my ideas and see what I should do:

My idea #1:   How many kinds of weeds grow in my yard?

First, I need to find a guidebook on weeds.
Second, I need to read about weeds in the library.
Third, I need to ask my parents for garden scissors or other old scissors to
use to cut the weeds and ask them to help me with the cutting.
Fourth, I need to find some heavy books to use to press my weeds so I will
be able to keep them.
Fifth, I need to hunt for different types of weeds in my yard once a week.

My idea #2:   How long does a light bulb last?

First, I need to read about light bulbs in the library.
Second, I need to ask my parents to help me find a lamp for a light bulb. I
want one that is safe to have turned on all the time.
Third, I need to decide what brand and what size of light bulb to use. I
could try several brands of the same size and compare the results.

WORKSHEET 2
PLANNING YOUR PROJECT

Now let's see what you need to do to plan your Science Fair Project.

WRITE YOUR IDEA AGAIN. _____

_____

WRITE WHAT YOU WILL COUNT OR MEASURE AGAIN. _____

_____

TO PLAN MY PROJECT:

First, I will need _____

_____

Second, I will need _____

_____

Third, I will need _____

_____

Fourth, I will need _____

_____

_____

STEP 5
SAFETY

Scientists are very, very careful when they work and do experiments. You will need to be very careful, too.

> DO NOT DO ANY EXPERIMENTING WITHOUT YOUR PARENTS.

Your teacher and your parents will go over the safety rules with you before you begin your Science Fair Project.

SAFETY RULES

1. Experimenting is serious work.
2. Do only those experiments approved by your teacher.
3. Keep your work area clean and uncluttered.
4. Never work alone. Always have one of your parents with you.
5. Use special caution when working with glass, matches, scissors, chemicals, and electricity.

WHEN YOU SEE THIS SYMBOL, **USE EXTRA CAUTION!**

6. Never play with plugs, switches, wall outlets, or light sockets or fixtures. The electricity from wall outlets is VERY dangerous.
7. Be careful with batteries. Use only AA, C or D batteries (1.5 volts). Sometimes even these batteries can make wires very hot.
8. Use only 1.5-volt light bulbs with AA, C or D batteries.

STEP 6
PLANNING TO GATHER YOUR DATA

Do you remember what I told you scientists call counting or measuring something in their experiments?
That's right. Data gathering.
Now you must plan how you will gather data and how you will keep a record of it.

Let's go back to my two ideas and see what I should do.

My idea #1:   How many kinds of weeds grow in my yard?

1. How often should I count the weeds?
   Once a week should be good.

2. How will I count the weeds?
   a] I will have my parents help me pull the weed out of the ground or cut it as close to the ground as we can.
   b] I will place the weed in a plastic sandwich bag and tape a piece of paper to it with a letter (A, B, C, etc.). Later I can find out what kind of weed it is.
   c] I will make a table like the one on the next page and write the date and the letter of the weed. I may need more rows in my table than this one has.

DATE	WEED TYPE (letter)	NUMBER FOUND
March 1	A	~~HHL~~ ~~HHL~~ I
March 1	B	~~HHL~~ I
March 1	C	~~HHL~~ III

d] I will count all the weeds of that type that I can find in my yard.

e] I will not need to dig up or cut every weed I find. I only need to dig up one example of each type of weed.

f] I will write the number of that type of weed I found in my yard on that day in the table.

g] I will repeat steps [a], [b], [d], and [f] for each different type of weed I can find in my yard. I will write the letter and the number of each of these weeds in my table.

3. How will I keep my weeds?

a] I will take each weed out of the plastic sandwich bag and carefully put it on a sheet of waxed paper.

b] I will tape its letter on the waxed paper.

c] I will carefully spread out the weed and place another sheet of waxed paper over it.

d] I will place this package between two heavy books.

4. How will I identify my weeds?

I will look for each one in the weed guidebook and write the name next to its letter in my table.

5. Are there any extra things I might want to do?

Maybe I could make a map of my yard and mark the places where I find each weed.

My idea #2: How long does a light bulb last?

1. How will I set up my experiment?

a] First, I will buy new light bulbs. My parents or my teacher will help me decide how many brands and sizes I should use.

b] Second, I will ask my parents to help me put the light bulbs in the lamps or light fixtures.

c] Third, I will ask my parents to help me turn on the lights at the same time.

2. How often should I check the light bulbs?

I should look at them several times a day to see if they have burned out. It would be best if I check them at the same times each day. Maybe I could make a schedule of times to check the light bulbs. I could try this schedule:

- 7 o'clock in the morning before I go to school
- 3 o'clock in the afternoon when I get home from school
- 8 o'clock at night before I go to bed

3. How will I record how long the light bulbs last?

I will use a table like the one below to mark the date I turned the lights on, the brand of light bulb, and when it burns out.

DATE STARTED	BRAND AND SIZE OF LIGHT BULB	DATE ENDED	TIME ENDED
March 1	Brand X - 100 watts	March 30	8 pm
March 1	Brand Z - 100 watts	April 22	7 am
March 1	Brand A - 100 watts	March 19	7 am

4. How many times should I try my experiment?

It would be best if I did my experiment several times. Usually light bulbs come in packages of 2 or 4, so I could repeat my experiment 2 or 4 times. Then I will have lots of data!

5. Are there any extra things I might want to do?

I could use several sizes of the same brand of light bulb.

WORKSHEET 3
PLANNING TO GATHER YOUR DATA

Now let's see what you need to do to gather data for your Science Fair Project.

WRITE WHAT YOU WILL COUNT OR MEASURE AGAIN _____

_____

TO PLAN TO RECORD MY DATA:

First, I will _____

_____

Second, I will _____

_____

Third, I will _____

_____

Fourth, I will need to use a table like the one below. If you have a computer in your classroom or at home, you may use it to make your data tables. Ask your teacher or your parents to show you how.

Use another piece of paper if you need to list more steps for your project.

STEP 7
GETTING READY

I'll bet you are anxious to get started with your Science Fair Project!

But first, we have just a few more things to do.

A scientist always has a "Controlled Experiment."

This means that only one thing is changed in the experiment.

Sometimes it means only counting things in one special place or measuring things after a certain amount of time.

Let's go back to my two ideas and see how we can make them "Controlled Experiments."

My idea #1:   How many kinds of weeds grow in my yard?

I will count only plants that my guidebook names as weeds and I will count only the weeds in my own yard.

My idea #2:   How long does a light bulb last?

The one thing that I will change is the brand of light bulb. I will make sure that all the light bulbs are all the same size.

Sometimes a Science Fair Project has two groups of plants or animals. You do something to one group, but not to the other. For example, you might give one group of plants fertilizer. This group is called the *Experimental Group* because you are experimenting on it. The other group is called the *Control Group* because you make sure not to do anything different to it. This way you can compare the results of the Experimental Group to the Control Group and you will know that what you did to the Experimental Group caused the difference.

WORKSHEET 4
GETTING READY

MAKING YOUR PROJECT A CONTROLLED EXPERIMENT

TO MAKE MY PROJECT A CONTROLLED EXPERIMENT, I WILL DO ONE OF THE FOLLOWING:

The one thing I will change is _____

_____

OR

I will count only the _____

in one special place, _____

OR

I will measure _____

after a certain amount of time, _____

IF I HAVE TWO GROUPS IN MY SCIENCE FAIR PROJECT:
    The group that I do something to is the Experimental Group.

    My Experimental Group is _____

    The group I do not do anything different to is the Control Group.

    My Control Group is _____

STEP 8
YOUR EXPERIMENTAL NOTEBOOK

I'm really excited about your Science Fair Project, aren't you? We've been planning a lot of things. That's what scientists do — a lot of planning first!

A scientist is very organized. One way a scientist keeps organized is by using an "Experimental Notebook."

A scientist keeps all of his or her ideas, notes, tables, and data in an Experimental Notebook.

Now, let's make our own Experimental Notebook. Put a check mark in the box when you have completed each of the steps below:

☐ We need to get a 3-ring notebook.

☐ We need to label the front of the notebook "Experimental Notebook."

☐ We will make a "Title Page." Put your name, your grade, and your teacher's name on this page. Then write the name of your Science Fair Project. The idea you wrote on page 30 can be your title for now. Later you can change it, if you want to.

☐ We will have our parents or teacher help us place the copy of some of the pages of this handbook into our Experimental Notebook. The pages we will need are pages 32, 38, and 40.

As you work on your Science Fair Project, you will add some more pages from this handbook to your Experimental Notebook.
I'll remind you with a picture like this ⇒

> **Put this page in your Experimental Notebook**

STEP 9
EXPERIMENTING

Here we go! Now that we have everything planned, we can actually begin experimenting!
We have to get all of our supplies together and find a time when our parents can help us.
We must follow our plans from Worksheets 2, 3, and 4.

You will need to make a larger copy of your data table from Worksheet 3. You may have to make two or three copies depending upon what you will be counting or measuring. Your teacher or parents can help you decide if you need other tables. Put these copies in you Experimental Notebook.

When you do any work on your Science Fair Project you should write it in your Experimental Notebook with the date and the day of the week. For example, yesterday I went to the library and read about weeds in an encyclopedia. I wrote that in my Experimental Notebook. Look on page 44 for an example of how to write notes in your Experimental Notebook.

Once your parents have helped you get started with your experimenting, set aside a certain time on several days of each week to work on your project. You may want to make a schedule to help you remember.

You may want to take photographs of what you do or what you find. Ask you parents if they can help you. I will ask my parents to take pictures of my yard and of the weeds when they are cut.

START TODAY; DON'T DELAY

STEP 10
YOUR REPORT

You picked your Science Fair Project because it was something you were curious about.

You have been experimenting to find out about your idea.

There is another important way to find out about your idea, too. READING!

You can find out a lot from books and encyclopedias.

Let's see what I could read about for my Science Fair Project.

My idea #1:   How many kinds of weeds grow in my yard?

I already have a guidebook to help me identify weeds, so I will read it. It tells me what a weed is, why it is called a weed, and some of the most common weeds. I will write this information in my Experimental Notebook along with the name of the guidebook and when the guidebook was published. I can look in the index of the guidebook to find the pages that tell about the kinds of weeds I have found in my yard. I will write the information I find on those pages in my Experimental Notebook.

I will write the Scientific Names of the weeds, too. All living things have been given a special name by scientists, a Scientific Name. It is usually in a language called Latin and it is often hard to pronounce and spell. Scientists use the Scientific Name because common, everyday names can be different in different countries and even in different parts of our own country! I will not worry about pronouncing these Scientific Names, but I will carefully copy them into my Experimental Notebook.

I will ask my teacher or the librarian to help me find some other books about weeds and some encyclopedia articles, too.

Now you have to do the same — look for books and encyclopedia articles that tell about the topic of your Science Fair Project.

You can set up your note pages in your Experimental Notebook like this:

THE NAME OF THE BOOK _____

THE AUTHOR _____

THE DATE THE BOOK WAS PUBLISHED _____

THE DATE I READ THE BOOK _____

WHAT INFORMATION I FOUND IN THE BOOK ABOUT
MY SCIENCE FAIR PROJECT

_____

_____

_____

_____

When you have read all you can, copy your notes from your Experimental Notebook into a report. Put a pretty cover on it. Maybe you can draw a picture on the cover that will show what your Science Fair Project is about. Your report will be part of your Science Fair Project when you take it to school for the Science Fair.

THE EXPERIMENTAL METHOD

Congratulations! Do you know what you've done? You have just followed the steps scientists use when they do experiments. These steps are called "The Experimental Method." Now let's see what the Experimental Method is.

THE EXPERIMENTAL METHOD	WHAT YOU HAVE ALREADY DONE
Purpose	Your idea on Worksheet 1
Procedure	Worksheet 2 "Planning Your Project," Worksheet 3 "Planning to Gather Data," Worksheet 4 "Getting Ready"
Experiment	What you have written in your Experimental Notebook
	WHAT YOU WILL DO SOON
Observations	What you will record in your data tables and what you will say about your data (Worksheet 5, "Understanding Your Data")
Conclusion	The "answer" to the question you asked in your idea (Worksheet 6, "Your Conclusion")

We will use the Experimental Method terms in our display later.

STEP 12
UNDERSTANDING YOUR DATA

Wow! You've completed your experiment and recorded your data.

Now you must figure out what your data tell you. You must make some observations about your data.

Let's look at some observations that I can make from the data from my experiment.

My idea #1:   How many kinds of weeds grow in my yard?

My Data Tables:

Table 1

DATE	WEED TYPE (letter)	NUMBER FOUND
March 1	thistle A	8
March 1	sourgrass B	6
March 1	plantain C	8
March 1	dandelion D	10
March 1	chickweed E	7

Table 2

DATE	WEED TYPE (letter)	NUMBER FOUND
March 8	thistle A	10
March 8	sourgrass B	11
March 8	plantain C	12
March 8	dandelion D	15
March 8	chickweed E	7

The rest of my data tables are on the next page.

The rest of my data tables are on the next page.

Table 3

DATE	WEED TYPE (letter)	NUMBER FOUND
March 15	thistle A	13
March 15	sourgrass B	13
March 15	plantain C	15
March 15	dandelion D	18
March 15	chickweed E	8

Table 4

DATE	WEED TYPE (letter)	NUMBER FOUND
March 22	thistle A	15
March 22	sourgrass B	15
March 22	plantain C	15
March 22	dandelion D	20
March 22	chickweed E	10

Table 5

DATE	WEED TYPE (letter)	NUMBER FOUND
March 29	thistle A	17
March 29	sourgrass B	16
March 29	plantain C	16
March 29	dandelion D	21
March 29	chickweed E	10

Table 6

DATE	WEED TYPE (letter)	NUMBER FOUND
April 5	thistle A	20
April 5	sourgrass B	18
April 5	plantain C	16
April 5	dandelion D	22
April 5	chickweed E	11

Did you notice that I changed the slash marks I used when I first filled in my tables to regular numbers?

To understand what my data tells me, I made another table for the last count of the number of each type of weed I found. This table is on the next page and shows the total number of each kind of weed I counted.

Table 7 - The Total Number of Weeds

WEED TYPE (letter)	TOTAL NUMBER FOUND
Thistle A	20
Sourgrass B	18
Plantain C	16
Dandelion D	22
Chickweed E	11
GRAND TOTAL	87

When I look at Table 7 with the totals, I find that the biggest number is 22 for weed D, dandelion. The smallest number is 11 for weed E, chickweed. The total number of weeds that I found in my yard is 87. These numbers are observations that I wrote in my Experimental Notebook.

My Observations:

I found 5 different types of weeds in my yard between March 1 and April 5. The types were: thistle, sourgrass, plantain, dandelion, and chickweed. I found a total of 87 weeds in my yard. The most common weed was dandelion (22). The least common weed was chickweed (11).

I used the data from my Table #7, The Total Number of Weeds, to explain what I found. The people who look at your Science Fair Project can see the data in the tables, but you must also explain it to them with words.

Get all of your data tables together and study them. You need to write an explanation of your data.

Here are some questions to guide you when you look at your data tables:

- Would a table with the total number help me?
- Did one thing happen the most?
- Did one thing happen the least?
- Would the average number help me?
- Did one kind change more than the others?
- Did all the things change in the same way?

You may want to ask your parents or teacher to help you understand your data.

Now, write the observations you can make from your data on the next page, Worksheet 5.

WORKSHEET 5
UNDERSTANDING YOUR DATA

Answer the following questions, if they apply to your Science Fair Project. You will probably not use all the questions.

What new data tables do I need to make?_____

Did one thing happen the most? _____

Did one thing happen the least? _____

Would the average number help me? _____

Did one kind change more than the others? _____

Did all the things change in the same way?_____

Now write your observations below:

_____

_____

_____

_____

_____

_____

_____

_____

| Put this page in your |
| Experimental Notebook |

STEP 13
MAKING GRAPHS

Your observations will be easier to understand if you make graphs of your data.

A graph shows the same data as your table, but in a different way.

There are two ways to make a graph. One is to make it by hand on graph paper and the other is to use a computer.

Your teacher and parents will help you decide which way to make your graphs.

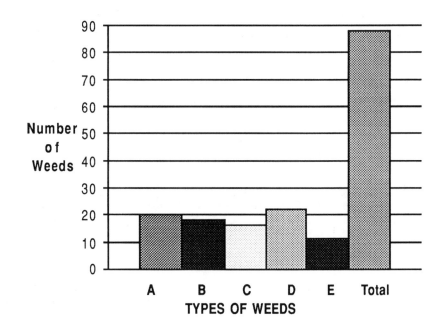

Total Number of Weeds in My Yard

Making Graphs by Hand

To make graphs by hand, you will need graph paper. This paper comes in many sizes. Your teacher may have some for you to use. If not, ask your parents to help you get some. Graph paper with 1-centimeter squares or 1/2-inch squares will probably be easiest for you to use.

Make a practice copy first. Place the paper the long way so that it matches this page. Print the title of your graph at the top. The title should tell what your graph shows. For my graph I will use the title "The Total Number of Weeds in my Yard."

TOTAL NUMBER OF WEEDS IN MY YARD

A graph has two sides, called axes. They are the dark lines on the left side and on the bottom of the graph above.

Each side, or axis, must have a label so that people will know what the graph means. On the left, or vertical, axis of my graph I will put the label "Number of Weeds." On the bottom, or horizontal, axis, I will put the label, "Types of Weeds" and the name each type of weed. This is how I started at my graph ⇓

TOTAL NUMBER OF WEEDS IN MY YARD

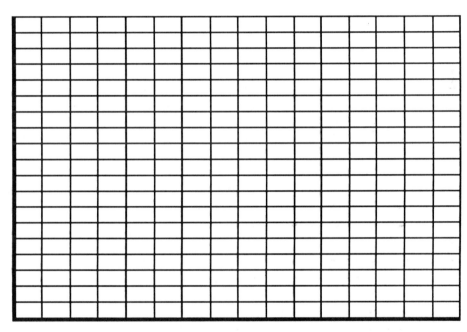

NUMBER OF WEEDS

Thistle   Sourgrass   Plantain   Dandelion   Chickweed

TYPES OF WEEDS

One of the easiest types of graphs to make is a bar graph like the one on page 51. A bar is the tower-like, shaded column shown here. ⇒
I will use one bar for each type of weed.

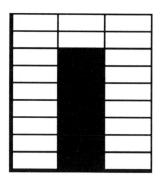

You will want to make your graph almost as large as the piece of graph paper.

I will leave some space on the left side of the graph to print my vertical axis label, "Number of Weeds," and some space at the bottom. Then I will draw the line for the vertical axis with a ruler.

piece
of
graph
paper

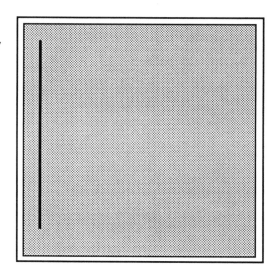

Next I will draw the line for the bottom, or horizontal axis, with a ruler.

piece
of
graph
paper

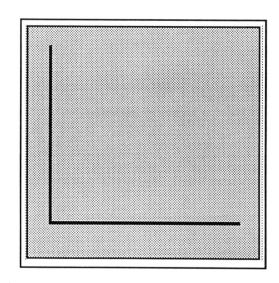

For the practice copy of my graph I can print the labels for the axes and the title in pencil. Later, on the "good" copy of my graph, I will use colored pencils or an erasable pen to print the labels and the title.

Since I want one bar for each type of weed, I will need 5 bars. I will space them evenly across the page. With only 5 bars on the graph, I will use the width of several squares of the graph paper for my bars. If the graph paper has 25 squares across its width, I may want to make each bar 3 squares wide.

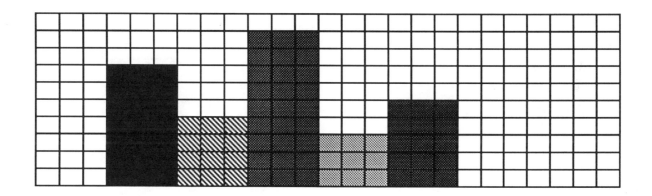

Later, I can decide if my graph would look neater if I leave some blank squares between the bars.

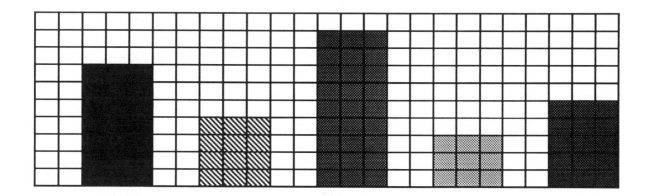

You can try different ways of placing the bars across the graph to find the one that will look best.

Under each 3-square bar I printed the name of the weed the bar will represent. Before we can figure out how tall to make my bars, I need to decide a scale to use for my graph. A scale tells how many weeds are counted in each square of my graph paper. For example, 1 square can stand for 1 weed or 1 square can represent 5 weeds. Let's see how these two different scales look:

If 1 square equals 1 weed, then the first bar will show 8 weeds. The second bar will show 3 weeds.

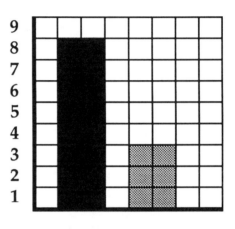

If 1 square equals 2 weeds, then the first bar will show 16 weeds. The second bar will represent 6 weeds.

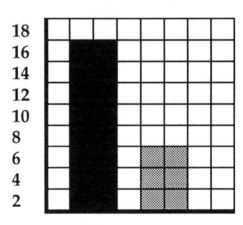

If 1 square equals 5 weeds, then the first bar in this graph shows 40 weeds. The second bar in this graph shows 15 weeds.

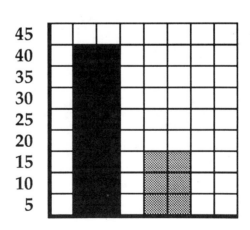

I asked my teacher to help me decide what scale to use for my graph. We looked at my data to find out what was the biggest number of weeds. There were 22 dandelions. Then we counted how many squares there are on the longest side of my graph paper and we found 27 squares. We need to leave about 3 squares for the horizontal axis label at the bottom. We decided to try a scale of 1 square for 1 weed. I started with the first square above the line I drew for the horizontal axis. Then I numbered only every other square so my numbers wouldn't be too crowded.

This shows part of the piece of graph paper that I used for my first practice graph. Since I want to show 20 thistles in the first bar, I counted up to the number 20 space in the 3 columns I chose to use for my first bar.

I printed the name of the weed below the columns. I will repeat these steps for each of my weeds.

Use a ruler to draw straight lines for the sides of each bar. After your practice graph looks the way you want it, make a "good" copy. You may color in each bar with a different colored pencil or ask your parents to help you cut a small strip of

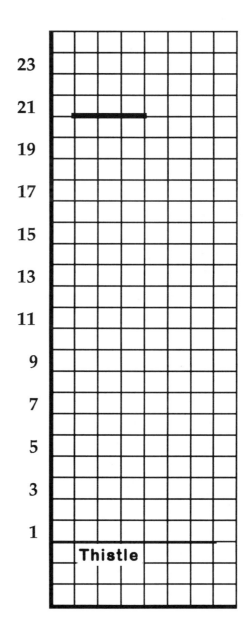

colored construction paper to fit in each bar. You can choose a different color for each bar and then paste them onto the graph. I am going to make a graph of each of my other data tables, too.

You can also use pictographs. A pictograph is a graph that has pictures instead of bars. If your project is about light bulbs, you could use a picture of a light bulb for each bar of your graph. You draw the picture to the height of that bar. Here is an example:

We will use the graphs we make on our displays. We'll work on our displays in Step 15.

Making Graphs with a Computer

If you have a computer in your classroom or at home, you may be able to make graphs with it. Ask your teacher or your parents to help you. There are many other types of graphs you can use to show your data. Computer programs often have many of these other types of graphs. You can try different graphs to see which one displays your data the best. Some examples of other types of graphs are shown on the next page.

a pie chart

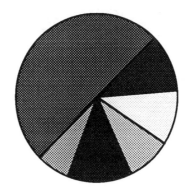

a line graph

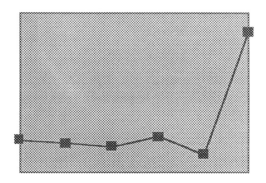

a 3-D bar
graph

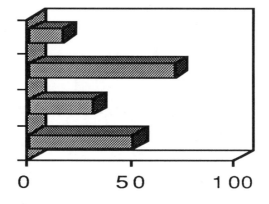

STEP 14
YOUR CONCLUSION

I'll bet you are very pleased that
    your experiment is done.
But, when something is finished,
    it should have an ending.
The end of a Science Fair Project
    is called the Conclusion.
The Conclusion is the "answer" to
    the question your idea asked.
Let's see what the Conclusion for
    my project will be.

My idea #1:   How many kinds of weeds grow in my yard?

My Conclusion is:

Five different types of weeds were found in my yard. They were
Thistle, Sourgrass, Plantain, Dandelion, and Chickweed. There
were a total of 87 weeds. Dandelions were the most common
weed in my yard.

Usually the conclusion is several sentences long. You want to give a
complete answer to the question you asked in your idea. Read your idea
again on Worksheet 1. Then think about what answer your data gives. I
asked "How many kinds of weeds grow in my yard?" My conclusion
answers this question by telling the different kinds of weeds I found and
how many weeds I found.

Write the conclusion for your Science Fair Project on Worksheet 6 on the
next page.

WORKSHEET 6
YOUR CONCLUSION

Write the Conclusion for your Science Fair Project.

_____

_____

_____

_____

_____

_____

_____

> **Put this page in your
> Experimental Notebook**

STEP 15
YOUR DISPLAY

Now you have a very fun part of your Science Fair Project to do. It's the display!

This is your chance to show all that you've done. And you can be as creative as you like.

A Science Fair Project needs to be displayed so everyone can see it and understand it.

The display has several parts:

•The Backboard
•The Props

•The Experimental Notebook
•The Report

Let's look at each part.

The Backboard.

This is the part of your display that will stand on the table that your teacher or the Science Fair Director provides. The backboard can have just one piece, like this:

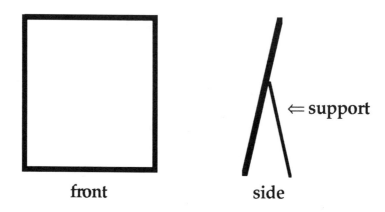

front   side

The backboard can have 2 sides, like this:

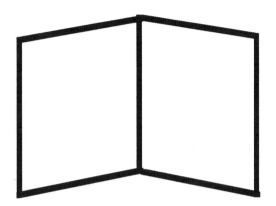

or three sides, like this:

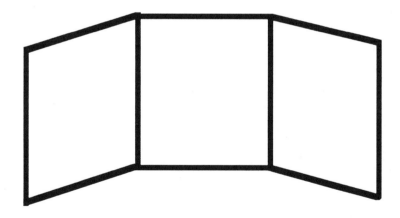

The backboard can be plain poster board or it can have some sort of frame. Ask your parents what kind they can help you make. The backboard needs to be sturdy. There are some kinds of backboards that you can buy. Your teacher may have some ideas, too.

One of the most important things about the backboard is that it is eye-catching. You can use colors to make your display stand out. Neatness is important, so plan everything before you cut or paste.

The first thing to plan is your title. You wrote a title on the first page of your Experimental Notebook. You can use that one or change the title. The title on your backboard must be large enough for everyone to see. You can use large stencils or a banner made on a computer. Your school may have a letter punch that you can use. You will use the terms and parts of the Experimental Method on your backboard. You will need to print or stencil the following headings:

- **PURPOSE**
- **PROCEDURE**

- **OBSERVATIONS**
- **CONCLUSION**

PURPOSE: You will use the idea you chose for your Science Fair Project for your Purpose. It is in Worksheet 1.

PROCEDURE: You will use what you have written on Worksheets 2, 3, and 4.

OBSERVATIONS: Your observations are your data tables from Worksheet 5, your explanation, and your graphs.

CONCLUSION: Worksheet 6 has your conclusion.

On the next page I'll show you what I will put on my display.

Here's what I will put on my display:

PURPOSE

How many kinds of weeds grow in my yard?

PROCEDURE

1. I cut one of each kind of weed as close to the ground as I could.
2. I put each of these weeds in a separate plastic bag and labeled it with a letter.
3. I recorded the letter of each weed and how many I found on each day in a data table.
4. I pressed one of each different type of weed and labeled it with its letter.
5. I identified each kind of weed with a weed guidebook.
6. I counted the weeds in my yard every week for six weeks.

OBSERVATIONS

(I attached my data tables and graphs here, then I wrote:)

I found five different types of weeds (thistle, sourgrass, plantain, dandelion, and chickweed) in my yard between March 1 and April 5. I found a total of 87 weeds in my yard. There were 22 dandelions. That was more than any other type of weed. There were only 11 chickweeds.

CONCLUSION

Five different kinds of weeds were found in my yard. They were thistle, sourgrass, plantain, dandelion, and chickweed. There was a total of 87 weeds. The most common weed was dandelion.

You may want to print each of the headings on a separate piece of poster-board or construction paper. Then you can paste or tape them onto your backboard. That way if you make a mistake on one heading, you will not ruin the whole display. It would be a good idea to do the same thing for the written part of your Purpose, Procedure, Observations, and Conclusion.

PURPOSE

How many kinds of weeds grow in my yard?

We want our displays to look especially nice, so I am going to use several colors of construction paper to mount these separate parts. If you have a computer in your classroom or at home, you can print out the headings and the written portion of each section. Then you can mount them on poster board on construction paper.

Be sure to allow at least two weeks to make your display. It takes lots of time and you may run into problems along the way. I ran out of paste right in the middle!

The Props

Props are parts of your experiment that you place on the table in front of your backboard. I will use the weeds I pressed. I will mount them on construction paper and label each one with it common name and its Scientific Name. I may also use my weed guidebook as a prop. If I want to use the photographs and the weed map of my yard, I can put them on the table or I can mount them on the backboard. Either way, I will first paste them on construction paper or poster board.

Your teacher or the Science Fair Director will tell you what things you will be allowed to use as props. Some things would not be save to have on the table with younger children coming to see your project. One more thing that might make your display stand out is a table cover or colored paper on the table.

The Experimental Notebook

You have this all ready! Just take it along and place it on the table. Don't worry if some pages are soiled or wrinkled or if you had to erase or cross something out. Scientists make mistakes when recording their data and sometimes have spills, too.

The Report

This is already done, too. Take it with you and place it on the table. Don't forget that a pretty cover on your report will make your display look even nicer.

This is what my display will look like:

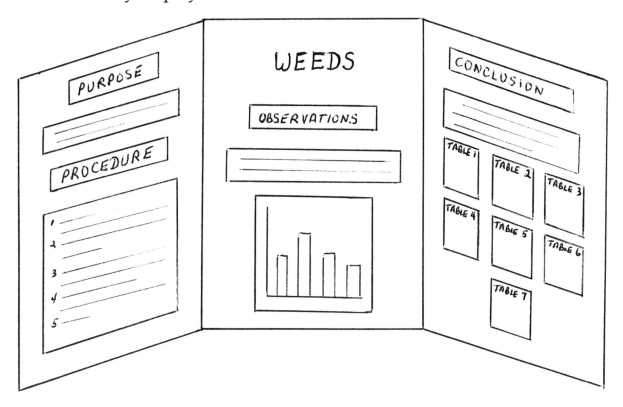

STEP 16
THE SCIENCE FAIR

I hope you enjoyed being a scientist. I did!

The only thing left to do is to take your project to the Science Fair. Your teacher will tell you when and where to go.

Be sure to tell your parents in plenty of time, so they can help you.

Take along some tape, paste, and scissors in case you need to fix something at the last minute. Use the checklist below to help you remember everything you need to take to the Science Fair:

☐ Backboard   ☐ Table cover
☐ Props   ☐ Tape
☐ Experimental Notebook   ☐ Paste
☐ Report   ☐ Scissors

If your Science Fair will have a judging session, you will want to dress neatly. Don't be scared; the judges just want you to tell them about your project. And that's easy, since you know everything you did. You might want to rehearse once or twice at home before the Science Fair. You can have your parents or older brother or sister ask you some questions about your project.

Good luck!
Have fun!
Maybe I'll see you next year for another Science Fair Project!

PART 3

SAMPLE PROJECTS AND PROJECT IDEAS

CHAPTER 4

Sample Projects and Project Ideas with Plants

This chapter (and each chapter in Part 3) contains two complete sample projects, a list of ideas for projects, and a list of children's literature about the chapter topic.

Each sample project has complete step-by-step instructions and answers for many of the worksheets. The child may use the answers provided and write them on his or her own worksheets. You and the student may have different answers that you want to use and may wish to modify the procedure.

The data gathering will be done by the student. Data tables are set up for ease of use and graph templates are provided. The student will need to complete the remainder of the worksheets and place them in the Experimental Notebook.

Additional ideas, props for the display, and resource books are suggested.

Sample Project #1

Idea: How much of a dandelion root must you pull out to keep the weed from growing again?

Background: People often pull up or dig out the dandelions in their yard. Usually the weeds seem to grow right back. Dandelions have one long main root (called a taproot) that may not be completely pulled out. You can find out if this is the reason dandelions seem to grow back so fast.

Books to read about this project:
>   an encyclopedia article on dandelions
>   a weed guidebook
>   an encyclopedia article about roots and taproots
>   bibliography, no. 31
>   bibliography, no. 32
>   bibliography, no. 50
>   bibliography, no. 60
>   bibliography, no. 63

WORKSHEET 1
PICKING YOUR PROJECT

What can you count or measure with your ideas?

Write below what you can count or measure for your ideas. Follow the examples I gave on what I could count or measure for my ideas.

1. For my idea # 1, I can count (or measure) *I will measure the size of the piece of root that will sprout a new dandelion plant.*

2. For my idea #2, I can count (or measure) _____

3. For my idea #3, I can count (or measure) _____

Which idea do you like best? Ask your parents or your teacher if they agree with you, then write the idea you chose on the lines below.

My idea for my Science Fair Project: *How much of a dandelion root must you pull out to keep the weed from growing again?*

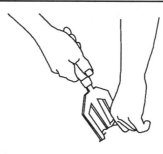

WORKSHEET 2
PLANNING YOUR PROJECT

Now let's see what you need to do to plan your
Science Fair Project.

Write your idea again. *How much of a dandelion*
root must you pull out to keep the weed from
growing again?

Write what you will count or measure again.
I will measure the size of the piece of root that will
sprout a new dandelion plant.

To plan my project:
First, I will need to READ *about dandelions and*
roots.

Second, I will need *to find where dandelions are*
growing in my yard and get my parents permission
to dig them up.

Third, I will need *to ask my parents to get a garden*
tool or something to use to dig up the dandelions.

Fourth, I will need *to get plastic storage bags to*
hold the dandelions I dig up.

Fifth, I will need *to get clear glass or plastic jars or*
old glasses to put the roots in to grow.

WORKSHEET 3
PLANNING TO GATHER YOUR DATA

Now let's see what you need to do to gather data on
your Science Fair Project.

Write what you will count or measure.
I will measure the size of the piece of root that will
sprout a new dandelion plant.

To plan to record my data:

First, I will *find where about 10 dandelions are*
growing in my yard.

Second, I will *get plastic storage bags to put the*
dandelions in.

Third, I will *get my parents to help me dig up the*
whole dandelion with all of its big root. This will
make quite a large hole.

Fourth, I will *have my parents help me take each*
dandelion and carefully cut away all of the plant
except the root.

Fifth, I will *measure the length of the root, put it*
back in its plastic bag, and label the plastic bag with
a letter. When I record the length of the root, I will
use the letter to know which measurement goes
with which root.

Sixth, I will *need to use a table like the one below.*
If you have a computer in your classroom or at home, you
may use it to make your data tables. Ask your teacher or
your parents to show you how.

Data Table

DANDELION	LENGTH OF WHOLE ROOT IN CENTIMETERS (cm)
A	20 cm
B	18 cm
C	22 cm
D	15 cm
E	20 cm
F	17 cm
G	18 cm
H	21 cm
I	20 cm
J	21 cm

Seventh, I will *get my parents to help me carefully*
cut away all of the root except a part of the
bottom. (See the diagram below.)

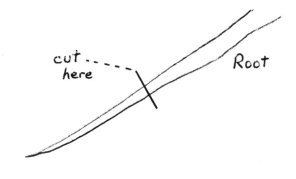

Eighth, I will *cut the bottom part of roots A and B to measure 3 centimeters.*

Ninth, I will *cut the bottom part of roots C and D to measure 6 centimeters.*

Tenth, I will *cut the bottom part of roots E and F to measure 9 centimeters.*

Eleventh, I will *cut the bottom part of roots G and H to measure 12 centimeters.*

Twelfth, I will *leave roots I and J whole.*

Thirteenth, I will *record the size of each root section and its size in the table below (Table 2).*

TABLE 2

DANDELION ROOT	LENGTH OF ROOT SECTION (in cm)	DID A PLANT GROW FROM THIS SECTION?
A	3 cm	
B	3 cm	
C	6 cm	
D	6 cm	
E	9 cm	
F	9 cm	
G	12 cm	
H	12 cm	
I	whole root (20 cm)	
J	whole root (21 cm)	

Fourteenth, I will *fill each jar almost full of water, cover each with plastic wrap or foil, and carefully punch a small hole in the center. I will label each jar with the letter of the root that will go into it.*

Fifteenth, I will *gently push the root section through the hole with the bottom tip of the root pointing down. I want to have most of the root in the water.*

Sixteenth, I will *label each jar with the letter and size of root section from my Table 2.*

Seventeenth, I will *check the roots each day to be sure there is enough water and to see if green parts have grown.*

Other ideas I can try:
- I can take photographs of:
  * the dandelions in my yard before I pick them,
  * the dandelions before I take off all the green parts,
  * the root sections I cut,
  * the jars with the roots in them at the beginning,
  * the roots at the end.
- I can use more dandelions.
- I can use more sizes of root sections.

WORKSHEET 4
GETTING READY

Making your project a controlled experiment

To make my project a controlled experiment, I will do one
of the following:

The one thing I will change is *the size of the dandelion*
root section I used.

I will count only the _____
in one special place, _____

I will measure _____
after a certain amount of time, _____

IF I HAVE TWO GROUPS IN MY SCIENCE FAIR PROJECT:
The group that I do something to is the Experimental Group.

My Experimental Group is *the different pieces of roots.*

The group I do not do anything different to is the Control
Group.
My Control Group is *the two whole roots.*

WORKSHEET 5
UNDERSTANDING YOUR DATA

Answer the following questions if they apply to your Science Fair Project. You will probably not use all the questions.

What new data tables do I need to make? _I do not need any other tables._

Did one thing happen the most? _I will tell which size root sections grew a new plant._

Did one thing happen the least? _No._

Would the average number help me? _No._

Did one kind change more than the others? _Not every size of root section grew a new plant._

Did all the things change in the same way? _No._

Now write your observations below:

_____

_____

Now you're on your own to complete your project —there's some help on the next pages, though!

Now you will make your graphs. You can use the example below.

New Dandelion Plants that Grew from Root Sections

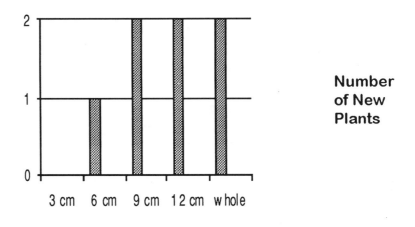

Number of New Plants

Size of Root Sections

Here are some ideas for your display:

- use photographs of the dandelions and the steps of your experiment on your backboard,
- use the jars and the root sections as props.

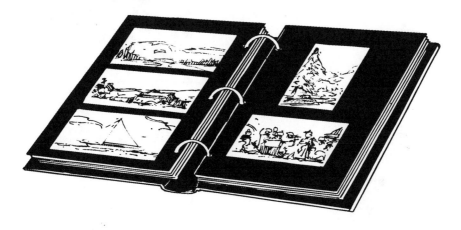

Sample Project #2

Idea: Do plants grow better with electricity?

Background: Plants need the energy from the sun to grow. Would the energy from electricity help them grow better? Could electricity in the soil help the plant get minerals? A safe way to find out is to use electricity made from the sun with a solar cell.

Books to read about this project:
    an encyclopedia article on solar energy cells
    a book on houseplants
    bibliography no. 31
    bibliography no. 19
    bibliography no. 41
    bibliography no. 50
    bibliography no. 59

WORKSHEET 1
PICKING YOUR PROJECT

What can you count or measure with your ideas?

Write below what you can count or measure for your ideas.
Follow the examples I gave on what I could count or
measure for my ideas.

1. For my idea # 1, I can count (or measure) *I will measure the height of the plant and the number of leaves.*

2. For my idea #2, I can count (or measure) _____

_____

3. For my idea #3, I can count (or measure) _____

_____

Which idea do you like best? Ask your parents or your teacher if they agree with you, then write the idea you chose on the lines below.

My idea for my Science Fair Project: *Do plants grow better with electricity?*

WORKSHEET 2
PLANNING YOUR PROJECT

Now let's see what you need to do to plan your
Science Fair Project.

Write your idea again. *Do plants grow better with*
electricity?

Write what you will count or measure again. *I will*
measure the height and the number of leaves on the
plants.

To plan my project:
First, I will need to READ *about electricity from solar*
cells and about houseplants.

Second, I will need *to find out where to buy a solar*
panel and plants that will grow well in my house.

Third, I will *need to find out how to hook up the*
solar panel.

Fourth, I will need *to ask my parents where I can*
grow my plants so that they will be safe and where
they will all get enough sunlight.

WORKSHEET 3
PLANNING TO GATHER YOUR DATA

Now let's see what you need to do to gather data on
your Science Fair Project.

Write what you will count or measure. _I will measure_
the height and the number of leaves on the plants.

To plan to record my data:
First, I will _ask my parents to buy 4 houseplants that_
are all about the same height and have about the
same number of leaves. I will ask the plant store
clerk if the plants need fertilizer and I will buy some
if my parents agree.

Second, I will _ask my parents to help me buy 2 small_
solar panels (size: approximately 1 x 3 inches and
200 millivolts), 22- or 24-gauge wire, and 4
galvanized or aluminum nails each about 3 inches
long.
NOTE: see _Appendix B_ for sources.

Third, I will _ask my parents to help me hook up the_
solar panels as in the diagram below.

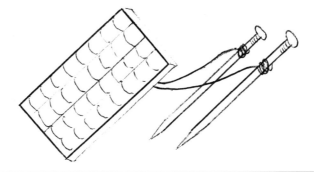

Fourth, I will _get two sticks to put the solar panels on_ _(old rulers, plant supports, or straight branches)._ _I can use duct tape to hold them on._

Fifth, I will _measure the height of each plant (in_ _centimeters) and count the number of leaves on each_ _plant. I will put labels on the pots._

Sixth, I will _use the measurements to pick two sets of_ _two plants that are the most alike._

Seventh, I will _need to use a table like the one below._ If you have a computer in your classroom or at home, you may use it to make your data tables. Ask your teacher or your parents to show you how.

PLANT	HEIGHT (in cm)	NUMBER OF LEAVES
A (without electricity)	10 cm	5
B (without electricity)	8 cm	4
C (with electricity)	10 cm	5
D (with electricity)	8 cm	4

Eighth, I will _put one solar panel on its stick in one_ _plant and the other solar panel in a second plant._ _The third and fourth plants will not get solar panels._

Ninth, I will _give all the plants the same amount of_ _water and fertilizer and keep all of them in the same_ _place._

Tenth, I will _make one new data table for each week._ _I will count the number of leaves and measure the_ _height of each plant each week. I will record the data_ _in the table for that week._

Other ideas I can try:
- I can take photographs of the plants,
- I can use more plants,
- I can use several different kinds of plants,
- I can use different sizes of solar panels.

WORKSHEET 4
GETTING READY

Making your project a controlled experiment

To make my project a controlled experiment, I will do one
of the following:

The one thing I will change is _if the plants get_
electricity from solar panels or if they do not.

I will count only the _____
in one special place, _____

I will measure _____
after a certain amount of time, _____

IF I HAVE TWO GROUPS IN MY SCIENCE FAIR PROJECT:
The group that I do something to is the Experimental Group.

My Experimental Group is _the two plants with the_
solar panels (and the electricity).

The group I do not do anything different to is the Control
Group.

My Control Group is _the two plants without the solar_
panels (and without electricity).

WORKSHEET 5
UNDERSTANDING YOUR DATA

Answer the following questions if they apply to your Science Fair Project. You will probably not use all the questions.

What new data tables do I need to make? *I will make a table of the increase in height of each plant and another table of the increase in the number of leaves.*

Did one thing happen the most? *I will tell whether the plants with electricity grew taller or had more leaves than the plants without electricity.*

Did one thing happen the least? *No.*

Would the average number help me? *The average height increase and the average increase in the number of leaves would help me.*

Did one kind change more than the others? *The plants with electricity grew more than the plants without electricity or the other way around.*

Did all the things change in the same way? *No.*

Now write your observations below:

_____

_____

_____

Now you will make your graphs. You can use the example below.

HEIGHT OF PLANTS

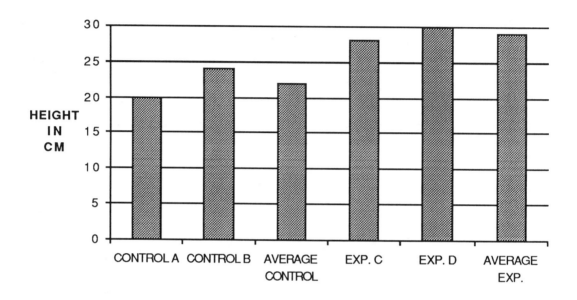

Here are some ideas for your display:
- use photographs of the plants on your backboard
- use the solar panels and the plants as props

Project Ideas with Plants

1. Can you make the buds of flowering trees and bushes bloom early?

Cut several twigs of different flowering trees and bushes during the winter and try to "force" them to bloom by bringing them indoors. Record how long each one takes and how successful you are.

2. How many seeds are on a dandelion?

Cut dandelions before the flowers make seeds and record the average number of the little parts that make up the yellow flower. Then cut dandelions when the seeds first appear, place them in plastic bags, and count the number of seeds. Compare the average number of flowers to the average number of seeds.

3. Do old seeds sprout as well as new seeds?

Find packages of seeds from last year (or years before) and compare the germination rate to new seeds. To find the germination rate, count an equal number (from 10 to 30) of old and new seeds of one type. Place them between layers of moistened paper towels in separate dishes, cover the dishes, and record how many seeds sprout in how many days.

4. Does the bark of all trees look the same?

Use a tree identification book to find different kinds of trees in your neighborhood. Tape tissue paper or tracing paper to each tree and rub the side of the lead of a #1 pencil or dark colored drawing chalk over the paper. Compare these "rubbings" of each kind of bark.

5. Does the color of light affect the germination rate of lettuce seeds?

Some seeds need light to sprout. Put seeds on moist paper towels under different colors of light and compare the number that sprout. You can use different colored light bulbs or colored cellophane taped over the open side of a box. Your control is "regular" sunlight.

6. Does old tea or gelatin really help plants grow?

Use either room temperature tea or a plain gelatin solution (you can buy this in the grocery store) to water houseplants that are all about the same size. Compare the growth of the plants after several weeks. Your control is a group of plants that are given plain water.

7. Do x-rays affect the germination rate of seeds?

Ask your dentist or doctor to x-ray some seeds. Place them on moistened paper towels and record the number that sprout and the time it takes. Your control is a group of the same seeds that are not x-rayed.

8. Does coconut milk have special plant growth chemicals in it?

Some plant scientists say that there are growth chemicals in coconut milk. You can get the milk from a fresh coconut and use different amounts in jars of distilled water to grow cuttings from houseplants. Your control is a group of the same kind and size of cuttings in distilled water alone.

9. Does a bigger seed make a better plant?

Measure the size of 20 to 30 dwarf sunflower seeds, bean seeds, or some other type of seed. Plant 5 of the largest seeds in the same conditions as 5 of the smallest seeds. Record the growth of the plants.

10. Can medicines help plants heal?

Make a cut in one leaf of each plant (or in several leaves of one plant if it is very large). Be sure all the cuts are the same size. Clean the scissors before using them for the next plant. Use one common medicine (iodine, merthiolate, antibiotic cream, alcohol, salve, aloe vera, plain bandage, medicated bandage, etc.) on each plant's wound. Your control is a plant with a cut, but no medicine at all. Take photographs after some cuts begin to heal. Record the time it takes each to heal.

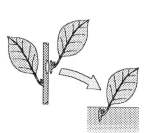

Children's Literature about Plants

Aliki. *A Weed Is a Flower: The Life of George Washington Carver.* Simon & Schuster, 1988.

Arnosky, Jim. *Crinkleroot's Guide to Knowing the Trees.* Branbury Press, 1989.

Bunting, Eve. *Someday a Tree.* Clarion, 1993.

Chesworth, Michael. *Archibald Frisby.* Farrar, Straus and Giroux, 1994.

Ehlert, Lois. *Planting a Rainbow.* Harcourt Brace Jovanovich, 1988.

Gibbons, Gail. *From Seed to Plant.* Holiday, 1991.

Hiscock, Bruce. *The Big Tree.* Atheneum, 1991.

King, Elizabeth. *Backyard Sunflower.* Dutton Children's Books, 1993.

Kite, Patricia. *Insect-Eating Plants.* Millbrook, 1995.

Lyon, George Ella. *A B Cedar: An Alphabet of Trees.* Orchard Books, 1989.

Markle, Sandra. *Outside and Inside Trees.* Bradbury, 1993.

Mettler, Rene. *Flowers.* Scholastic, 1993.

Moore, Elaine. *Grandma's Garden.* Lothrop, Lee & Shepard, 1994.

Muller, Gerda. *Around the Oak.* Dutton Children's Books, 1994.

Ryder, Joanne. *Hello, Tree!* Dutton/Lodestone, 1991.

Shannon, George. *Seeds.* Houghton Mifflin, 1994.

Wexler, Jerome. *Wonderful Pussy Willows.* Dutton, 1992.

CHAPTER 5

Sample Projects and Project Ideas with Animals and Insects

This chapter (and each chapter in Part 3) contains two complete sample projects, a list of ideas for projects, and a list of children's literature about the chapter topic.

Each sample project has complete step-by-step instructions and answers for many of the worksheets. The child may use the answers provided and write them on his or her own worksheets. You and the student may have different answers that you want to use and may wish to modify the procedure.

The data gathering will be done by the student. Data tables are set up for ease of use and graph templates are provided. The student will need to complete the remainder of the worksheets and place them in the Experimental Notebook.

Additional ideas, props for the display, and resource books are suggested.

Sample Project #3

Idea: Are cats "right-handed"?

Background: Most people are right-handed. Scientists say that chickens, monkeys, mice, and toads use one hand or foot or paw more than the other. You can find out if cats use their right paw or their left paw more often.

Books to read about this topic:

        an encyclopedia article on cats
        an encyclopedia article on handedness
        bibliography, no. 37
        bibliography, no. 50

WORKSHEET 1
PICKING YOUR PROJECT

What can you count or measure with your ideas?

Write below what you can count or measure for your ideas. Follow the examples I gave on what I could count or measure for my ideas.

1. For my idea # 1, I can count (or measure) *I will count the number of cats I test that are right-handed and the number that are left-handed.*

2. For my idea #2, I can count (or measure)_____
_____

3. For my idea #3, I can count (or measure) _____
_____

Which idea do you like best? Ask your parents and your teacher if they agree with you, then write the idea you chose on the lines below.

My idea for my Science Fair Project: *Are cats right-handed?*

WORKSHEET 2
PLANNING YOUR PROJECT

Now let's see what you need to do to plan your
Science Fair Project.

Write your idea again. _Are cats right-handed?_

Write what you will count or measure again.
I will count the number of cats I test that are right-handed and the number that are left-handed.

To plan my project:
First, I will need to READ _about cats and about how people are right-handed or left-handed._

Second, I will need _to ask my neighbors and my grandparents if I can test their cats. And I will need to ask Mom and Dad if it is OK to test our cat, too._

Third, I will need _a jar to put a cat treat in to make the cat try reach the snack with only one paw._

Fourth, I will need _to find a way to keep the jar from rolling around and to keep the cat from picking up the jar._

WORKSHEET 3
PLANNING TO GATHER YOUR DATA

Now let's see what you need to do to gather data on your Science Fair Project.

Write what you will count or measure. *I will count the number of cats I test that are right-handed and the number that are left-handed.*

To plan to record my data:
First, I will *get permission and make a list of the names of all the cat"volunteers" from their owners.*

Second, I will *get a square-type instant coffee jar from my mom. I will check to see if it is heavy enough so that the cat cannot move it.*

Third, I will *find a cat snack that all the cats like.*

Fourth, I will *need to use a table like the one below.*
If you have a computer in your classroom or at home, you may use it to make your data tables. Ask your teacher or your parents to show you how.

CAT NAME	TIMES CAT USED RIGHT PAW	TIMES CAT USED LEFT PAW

Fifth, I will *make a schedule of when I will test the cats. Only one test each day because I do not want the cats to get too used to reaching in the jar. I will need to have an adult with me when I test the cats.*

Sixth, I will *test each cat 5 times.*

Seventh, I will *test the cats in a quiet room that they are used to. I will put the snack in the jar, put the jar on the floor, and go a little way out of the room. I will stay where I can see what the cat does.*

Eighth, I will *not count the test if the cat does not try to get the treat.*

Other ideas I can try:
- I can take photographs of each cat volunteer and maybe take a picture of one of the cats reaching into the jar to get the treat.
- I can try to find out how many people are right-handed and how many are left-handed.
- I can try to find out if anyone knows about animals being right-handed.
- I can use my data to figure out the percentage of the cats I tested that are right-handed and left-handed.

WORKSHEET 4
GETTING READY

Making your project a controlled experiment

To make my project a controlled experiment, I will do one
of the following:

The one thing I will change is _____

OR

I will count only the *paw the cat uses first to reach*
into the jar. _____

in one special place, _____

OR

I will measure _____
after a certain amount of time, _____

IF I HAVE TWO GROUPS IN MY SCIENCE FAIR PROJECT:
The group that I do something to is the Experimental Group.

My Experimental Group is _____

The group I do not do anything different to is the Control
Group.

My Control Group is _____

WORKSHEET 5
UNDERSTANDING YOUR DATA

Answer the following questions if they apply to your Science Fair Project. You will probably not use all the questions.

What new data tables do I need to make? *I will make a table with the number of cats that are right-handed or left-handed.*

Did one thing happen the most? *Right-handed or left-handed...*

Did one thing happen the least? *Right-handed or left-handed...*

Would the average number help me? *No.*

Did one kind change more than the others? *No.*

Did all the things change in the same way? *No.*

Now write your observations below:

_____

_____

_____

Now you're on your own to complete your project —there's some help on the next pages, though!

Now you will make your graphs. You can use the example below.

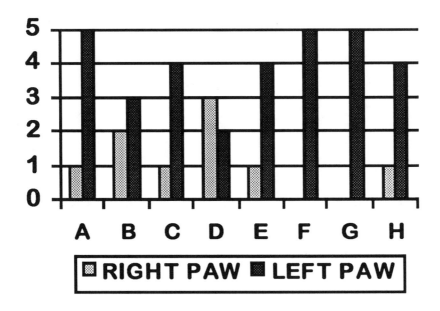

**RIGHT-HANDED AND LEFT-HANDED
TRIALS WITH EIGHT CATS**

Here are some ideas for your display:
- use photographs of the cats on your backboard,
- use the jar as a prop,
- use a toy stuffed cat to show how the real cats reached into the jar.

Sample Project #4

Idea: How fast can ants find food?

Background: When one ant finds some food, it returns to the ant hill to tell the other ants where to go to find the food, too. Do all the ants take the same amount of time to find the food as the first ant or are they faster? You can use an ant farm or an ant hill outside to find out.

Books to read about this topic:
  an encyclopedia article on ants
  how to make an ant farm (an ant farm is also called a formicarium)
  bibliography, no. 10
  bibliography, no. 50

WORKSHEET 1
PICKING YOUR PROJECT

What can you count or measure with your ideas?

Write below what you can count or measure for your ideas.
Follow the examples I gave on what I could count or
measure for my ideas.

1. For my idea # 1, I can count (or measure) _I will_
measure how long it takes the ants to find the food.

2. For my idea #2, I can count (or measure)_____

3. For my idea #3, I can count (or measure) _____

Which idea do you like best? Ask your parents and your
teacher if they agree with you, then write the idea you
chose on the lines below.

My idea for my Science Fair Project: _How long does it_
take ants to find food?

WORKSHEET 2
PLANNING YOUR PROJECT

Now let's see what you need to do to plan your
Science Fair Project.

Write your idea again. *How long does it take ants to*
find food?

Write what you will count or measure again. *I will*
measure how long it takes the ants to find the food.

To plan my project:
First, I will need to READ *about ants.*

Second, I will need *to find where there is an ant hill*
near my house or if I can buy or make an ant farm.

Third, I will need *to ask my parents if I can use a*
watch with a second hand or a stopwatch.

WORKSHEET 3
PLANNING TO GATHER YOUR DATA

Now let's see what you need to do to gather data on your Science Fair Project.

Write what you will count or measure. _I will measure how long it takes the ants to find the food._

To plan to record my data:

First, I will _find where there is an ant hill near my house or if I can buy or make an ant farm._

*NOTE: Appendix B lists places to buy an ant farm. Many other books tell how to make an ant farm (including bibliography no. 10.

Second, I will _find out what these ants like to eat. Some ants like sugar and some like grease. I will ask one of my parents to help me make a very thick mixture of sugar in water. I will place this about a foot away from the ant hill (or in the ant farm). I will watch if the ants come to eat the sugar. If they don't, I will try grease. I will ask my parents for some bacon grease or a bit of meat fat. I will put this near the ant hill (or in the ant farm) and see if the ants come to eat it._

Third, I will _get the watch or clock with a second hand or the stopwatch that my parents have said I may use._

Fourth, I will _need to learn how to use the watch, clock, or stopwatch._

Fifth, I will *need to use a table like the one below.*
If you have a computer in your classroom or at home, you may use it to make your data tables. Ask your teacher or your parents to show you how.

ANT	TIME (IN MINUTES AND SECONDS)
1	
2	
3	
4	
5	
6	
7	
8	
9	
10	

Sixth, I will *make a table like the one above for each test I do. I should do at least 10 tests.*

Seventh, I will *ask my mother or my sister if I may use some bright colored nail polish to mark the first ant on its legs (this will not hurt the ant).*

Eighth, I will *place a little bit of the food the ants like near the ant hill (or in the ant farm) and time how long it takes the first ant to find the food. I will record the time in minutes and seconds in my data table.*

Ninth, I will *mark the ant's legs with a little bit of the nail polish while it is eating.*

Tenth, I will *watch for other ants to come from the ant hill to the food and measure how long it takes from the time they come out of the ant hill until they find the food. I will record the time in minutes and seconds in my data table.*

Eleventh, I will *put the food in different places for each of my other tests. I will wait a day or two before doing another trial.*

Other ideas I can try:
- I can take photographs of the ants, the ant hill, or the ant farm.
- I can do more trials.
- I can use several different ant hills.
- I can put obstacles in the ants' way.
- I can try to figure out a way to measure or draw the paths the ants follow.

WORKSHEET 4
GETTING READY

Making your project a controlled experiment

To make my project a controlled experiment, I will do one of the following:

The one thing I will change is _____

I will count only the *time from when the ant first comes out of its hill until it finds the food* in one special place, _____

I will measure _____
after a certain amount of time, _____

IF I HAVE TWO GROUPS IN MY SCIENCE FAIR PROJECT:
The group that I do something to is the Experimental Group.

My Experimental Group is _____

The group I do not do anything different to is the Control Group.

My Control Group is _____

WORKSHEET 5
UNDERSTANDING YOUR DATA

Answer the following questions if they apply to your Science Fair Project. You will probably not use all the questions.

What new data tables do I need to make? *I should make a table of the average times for the second ant, the third ant, and so on.*

Did one thing happen the most? *I will tell whether the ants get faster or slower.*

Did one thing happen the least? *No.*

Would the average number help me? *Yes.*

Did one kind change more than the others? *Did some of the ants get faster, but not all?*

Did all the things change in the same way? *No.*

Now write your observations below:

_____

_____

Now you're on your own
to complete your project
—there's some help on
the next pages, though!

Now you will make your graphs. You can use the example below.

Time Needed for Ants to Find Food

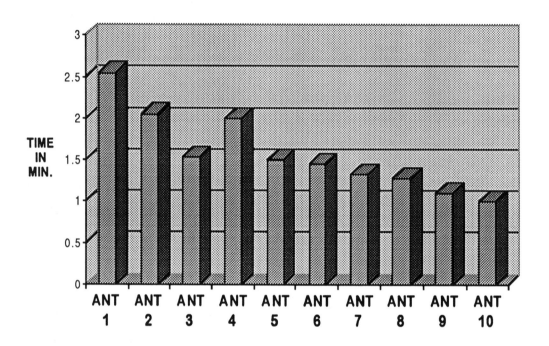

Here are some ideas for your display:
- use photographs of the ants, ant hill, or ant farm on your backboard.
- use photographs of the steps of your experiment on your backboard.
- use the ant farm prop (you may not be allowed to have the ants inside the ant farm; ask your teacher).
- use toy ants as props.

Project Ideas with Animals and Insects

1. Do vitamins affect the growth of tadpoles?

Collect or buy frog eggs and add 1 vitamin A tablet to 1 gallon of the water you keep the eggs in. Your control is a set of eggs in the same water but without the vitamin. Record the time it takes for the tadpoles to emerge from the eggs. Record the development of the tadpoles.

2. Does a cricket's chirp change with the temperature?

Count the number of chirps a cricket makes each evening and record the outdoor temperature. Make a graph to compare the number of chirps and the temperatures. Carefully catch a few crickets, identify what kind they are, and release them.

3. What kinds of butterflies visit your backyard?

Record the types and numbers of butterflies you observe in your yard. Do not catch or touch them. Make a record of what kinds visit other places in your county, such as a park or a farm.

4. Can goldfish learn?

Train goldfish with a signal when you feed them. You can tap once or twice on the bowl just before you give them food or turn on the lights or play music. Always place the food in the same part of the bowl. After training them for several weeks, try giving the signal without the food. See if the goldfish come to the feeding station.

5. What kinds of birds come to your bird feeder?

Use a bird identification book to keep a record of the kinds of birds that eat at your bird feeder. You can try this with different kinds of bird food or with suet. Try taking photographs of some of the birds that visit your feeder.

6. Do all colors of light attract the same kinds of insects?

Use different colored light bulbs in an outdoor lamp and build an insect trap. Record the kinds and numbers of insects you catch with each color of light.

7. Does the amount of salt affect the size of a population of brine shrimp?

Fish and pet stores sell brine shrimp as food for certain fish. You can buy a kit to grow brine shrimp. Use different amounts of the salt provided and record the number of brine shrimp in each. You can use a piece of paper with a black line drawn on it to make a comparison of how dense the population of brine shrimp is. Your control is a population grown in the amount of salt the kit describes.

8. Does music affect the amount of food hamsters eat?

You will need at least 4 hamsters, gerbils, or other small pets. Play music for one pair and record the amount of food and water they eat and drink. Your control is the other pair that has no music played for them.
NOTE: It is best to use hamsters, gerbils, or rats. They do not make their cages as smelly as mice do.

9. Will a lightning bug come when called?

When lightning bugs, or fireflies, blink their lights they are looking for other lightning bugs. They find each other by flashing light signals back and forth. Use a stopwatch to time how long a lightning bug's blink is and how long there is between blinks. Use a flashlight to copy the blinks and record how many lightning bugs come toward you. You can also record how long it takes the lightning bugs to come. See if your timing works the same way on another night.

10. Can gerbils survive jet lag?

Your parents probably won't let you take the gerbils on an airplane trip across the country, but you can study jet lag anyway. Scientists say that jet lag makes us tired, grumpy, and makes our stomachs hungry at the wrong time when we travel to different time zones. You can test the changes in how gerbils eat, sleep, and behave with jet lag. You will make jet lag by changing around their day and night. First, watch four gerbils for a week to see how they behave, measure how much they eat and drink, and how long and at what time they sleep. Keep 2 gerbils in normal day and night. Then put the other 2 gerbils in a place where you can control the light, such as a large closet. Use a timer to have the light come on during regular nighttime and turn off during the day. Record their behavior during their "day," how much they eat and drink, and when they sleep.

Children's Literature about Animals and Insects

Aliki. *My Visit to the Aquarium.* HarperCollins, 1993.

Arnosky, Jim. *Crinkleroot's Book of Animal Tracking.* Branbury, 1989.

Arnosky, Jim. *Crinkleroot's 25 More Animals Every Child Should Know.* Branbury, 1989.

Arnosky, Jim. *Every Autumn Comes the Bear.* G. P. Putnam's Sons, 1993.

Arnosky, Jim. *A Kettle of Hawks and Other Wildlife Groups.* G. P. Putnam's Sons, 1993.

Auch, Mary Jane. *Bird Dogs Can't Fly.* Holiday House, 1993.

Burton, Jane. *See How They Grow: Chick.* Dutton/Lodestone, 1992.

Charles, Donald. *Ugly Bug.* Dial, 1994.

Clark, Margaret Goff. *The Endangered Florida Panther.* Dutton/Penguin, 1993.

DaVolls, Linda. *Tano & Binti: Two Chimpanzees Return to the Wild.* Clarion, 1994.

Desmuth, Patricia. *Those Amazing Ants.* Macmillan, 1994.

French, Vivian. *Caterpillar, Caterpillar.* Candlewick, 1993.

Gallardo, Evelyn. *Among the Orangutans: The Birute Galdikas Story.* Chronicle, 1993.

Goodall, Jane. *The Chimpanzee Family Book.* Simon & Schuster, 1989.

Gove, Doris. *One Rainy Night.* Atheneum, 1994.

Grahm-Barber, Lynda. *Toad or Frog, Swamp or Bog.* Four Winds, 1994.

Hendrick, Mary Jean. *If Anything Ever Goes Wrong At the Zoo....* Harcourt Brace Jovanovich, 1993.

Kendall, Martha E. *John James Audubon: Artist of the Wild.* Millbrook, 1993.

Martin, Jacquelin Briggs. *Good Times on Grandfather Mountain.* Orchard Books, 1992.

MacAlary, Florence. *You Can Be a Woman Marine Biologist.* Cascade, 1993.

Oram, Hiawyn. *A Creepy Crawly Song Book.* Farrar, Straus and Giroux, 1993.

Parker, Nancy Winslow. *Working Frog.* Greenwillow, 1992.

Rydet, Joanne. *One Small Fish.* Morrow Junior Books, 1993.

Sage, James. *Where the Great Bear Watches.* Viking, 1993.

Yolen, Jane. *Animal Fare.* Harcourt Brace Jovanovich, 1994.

CHAPTER 6

Sample Projects and Project Ideas in Chemistry

This chapter (and each chapter in Part 3) contains two complete sample projects, a list of ideas for projects, and a list of children's literature about the chapter topic.

Each sample project has complete step-by-step instructions and answers for many of the worksheets. The child may use the answers provided and write them on his or her own worksheets. You and the student may have different answers that you want to use and may wish to modify the procedure.

The data gathering will be done by the student. Data tables are set up for ease of use and graph templates are provided. The student will need to complete the remainder of the worksheets and place them in the Experimental Notebook.

Additional ideas, props for the display, and resource books are suggested.

Sample Project #5

Idea: Why do you have to put vinegar in the dye when you color eggs?

Background: People all over the world color eggshells. Some make colorful eggs at Easter. Many of the ways to dye eggshells tell you to add vinegar to the dye. What happens if you don't?

Books to read about this project:
>   an encyclopedia article on Easter eggs
>   an encyclopedia article on dyes
>   bibliography no. 18
>   bibliography no. 35
>   bibliography no. 43
>   bibliography no. 50
>   bibliography no. 59

WORKSHEET 1
PICKING YOUR PROJECT

What can you count or measure with your ideas?

Write below what you can count or measure for your ideas. Follow the examples I gave on what I could count or measure for my ideas.

1. For my idea # 1, I can count (or measure) *the color of eggs dyed with different amounts of vinegar in the dye.*

2. For my idea #2, I can count (or measure)_____

_____

3. For my idea #3, I can count (or measure) _____

_____

Which idea do you like best? Ask your parents or your teacher if they agree with you, then write the idea you chose on the lines below.

My idea for my Science Fair Project: *Why do you have to put vinegar in the dye when you color eggs?*

WORKSHEET 2
PLANNING YOUR PROJECT

Now let's see what you need to do to plan your
Science Fair Project.

Write your idea again. *Why do you have to put vinegar*
in the dye when you color eggs?

Write what you will count or measure again. *I will show*
the color of eggs dyed with different amounts of
vinegar in the dye.

To plan my project:

First, I will need to READ *about dyeing Easter eggs.*

Second, I will need *to get Easter egg dye or two large*
(1-ounce or 29-mL) bottles of liquid food coloring
(in the spice or cake decorating aisle of the grocery
store), eggs, and white vinegar. The red dye will
work best, but I may want to try other colors.

Third, I will need *to ask my parents for 12 old glass jars*
(big enough to hold an egg), measuring spoons, a
measuring cup, and a large container (about 1 gallon).

WORKSHEET 3
PLANNING TO GATHER YOUR DATA

Now let's see what you need to do to gather data on your Science Fair Project.

Write what you will count or measure. *I will show the color of eggs dyed with different amounts of vinegar in the dye.*

To plan to record my data:

First, I will *get the dye, 1 dozen eggs, vinegar, 12 old glass jars, measuring spoons, and measuring cup.*

Second, I will *I will ask my parents whether they want me to use hard-cooked eggs or unboiled eggs for my experiment (either will work just fine). My parents will have to cook the eggs for me.*

Third, I will *put old newspapers on the kitchen table or wherever my parents tell me I can work.*

Fourth, I will *carefully pour both bottles of food coloring into the large container and carefully add 12 cups of room-temperature water (about 70° F or 20° C).*

Fifth, I will *have my parents help me put about 1 cup of the dye into each old jar.*

Sixth, I will *label each jar with the amount of vinegar I put in it (see the table on the next page).*

Amount of Vinegar in Each Jar

JAR	AMOUNT OF VINEGAR (in teaspoons)	JAR	AMOUNT OF VINEGAR (in teaspoons)
A	0	G	3
B	1/2	H	3 1/2
C	1	I	4
D	1 1/2	J	4 1/2
E	2	K	5
F	2 1/2	L	5 1/2

Seventh, I will *put one egg in each jar for 10 minutes.*

Eighth, I will *carefully take each egg out after the 10 minutes and dip it 4 times in a jar of clear water.*

Ninth, I will *wash and dry each jar and make sure the label is still attached.*

Tenth, I will *let each egg dry at room temperature in the clean dry jar it was dyed in.*

Eleventh, I will *arrange the dry eggs according to the color. I will put the darkest one first, then the next darkest, down to the lightest. I will be careful to keep each egg with its labeled jar.*

Other ideas I can try:
- I can take photographs of the dyed eggs to show the difference in color.
- I can use different colors of dye.
- I can measure the pH of the different vinegar solutions.
- I can try the same experiment with natural dyes.
- I can use the same amount of vinegar with different amounts of the dye.

WORKSHEET 4
GETTING READY

Making your project a controlled experiment

To make my project a controlled experiment, I will do one
of the following:

The one thing I will change is *amount of vinegar*

I will count only the _____
in one special place, _____

I will measure _____
after a certain amount of time, _____

IF I HAVE TWO GROUPS IN MY SCIENCE FAIR PROJECT:
The group that I do something to is the Experimental Group.

My Experimental Group is *all the jars except A.*

The group I do not do anything different to is the Control
Group.

My Control Group is *jar A with no vinegar.*

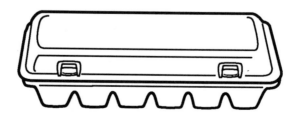

WORKSHEET 5
UNDERSTANDING YOUR DATA

Answer the following questions if they apply to your Science Fair Project. You will probably not use all the questions.

What new data tables do I need to make? *I will not need any other data tables.*

Did one thing happen the most? *The eggs with the most vinegar ...*

Did one thing happen the least? *The eggs with no vinegar ...*

Would the average number help me? *No.*

Did one kind change more than the others? *I will tell which amount of vinegar made the darkest color.*

Did all the things change in the same way? *No.*

Now write your observations below:

_____

_____

_____

Now you're on your own to complete your project —there's some help on the next pages, though!

You will not need graphs for this Science Fair Project.

Here are some ideas for your display:
- use photographs of the colored eggs on your backboard,
- use the actual colored eggs as props
  (you may be able to find jars with openings that will just fit the eggs so that you can stand them on top of the jars),
- use egg cartons to hold the eggs,
- build a riser or tiered stand to show the eggs,
- use an empty vinegar bottle and the empty dye bottles.

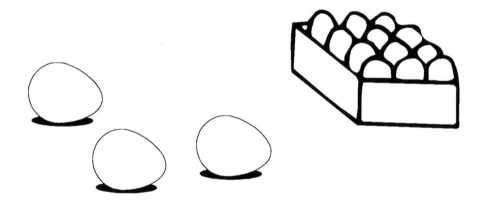

Sample Project #6

Idea: How are the colors in candies made?

Background: There are many bright colors used in candy and they are sometimes made with the same food dyes you have in your kitchen. You can find out which dyes are used to make blue M&M® candies and purple Skittles® candies.

Books to read about this project:
> an encyclopedia article on food dyes
> an encyclopedia article on candy-making
> books about chromatography such as:
>> bibliography no. 2
>> bibliography no. 35
>> bibliography no. 50

WORKSHEET 1
PICKING YOUR PROJECT

What can you count or measure with your ideas?

Write below what you can count or measure for your ideas. Follow the examples I gave on what I could count or measure for my ideas.

1. For my idea # 1, I can count (or measure) _I will count the food dyes in the candy._

2. For my idea #2, I can count (or measure)_____

3. For my idea #3, I can count (or measure) _____

Which idea do you like best? Ask your parents or your teacher if they agree with you, then write the idea you chose on the lines below.

My idea for my Science Fair Project: _What food dyes are used to make the colors in candy?_

WORKSHEET 2
PLANNING YOUR PROJECT

Now let's see what you need to do to plan your
Science Fair Project.

Write your idea again. _What food dyes are used to make_
the colors in candy?

Write what you will count or measure again. _I will count_
the food dyes in candies.

To plan my project:

First, I will need to READ _about food dyes._

Second, I will need _to get M&M® and Skittles®_
candies, toothpicks, food dyes, 7 glass jars or plastic
cups that are about 6 inches tall, and 13 small plastic
saucers or plastic lids.

Third, I will _need to get 7 cone-shaped coffee filters or_
7 pieces of filter paper.

NOTE to Parents: The local high school may give you
filter paper (15-cm discs or 15-cm squares).

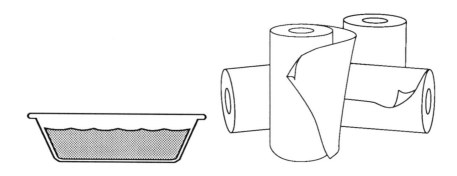

WORKSHEET 3
PLANNING TO GATHER YOUR DATA

Now let's see what you need to do to gather data on
your Science Fair Project.

Write what you will count or measure. *I will count the*
food dyes used to make the colors in candy.

To plan to record my data:

First, I will *use M&M® and Skittles® candies*

Second, I will *have an adult help me cut the filter*
paper or coffee filters into seven 2-inch by 5-inch
squares. I will try not to put my fingers on the part
of the paper that I will be using for the experiment.

Third, I will *draw a line with a pencil 1/4 inch from*
the thin edge of each paper and mark the names of
the colors below the line (also with a pencil).

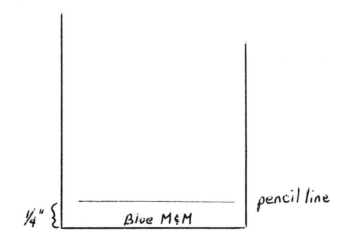

Fourth, I will *put old newspaper on my work space.*

Fifth, I will *mix 1/4 teaspoon of table salt in 4 cups of water.*

Sixth, I will *put one candy of each different color on a separate saucer and put one or two drops of the saltwater on each candy.*

Seventh, I will *have the adult who is helping me carefully push one end of each of 13 toothpicks hard on the table to mash them into little "brushes."*

Eighth, I will *wait about 30 minutes until the colors are coming off of the candies and then dip a toothpick "brush" into the color.*

Ninth, I will *dot the toothpick on the line I drew on one of the filter papers above the name of the color I am using. I will try to keep the dot very small.*

Tenth, I will *repeat steps 8 and 9 for each color and I will use a different toothpick for each color.*

Eleventh, I will *put one or two drops of each of the food dyes in a separate saucer and use a separate toothpick to dot each color on the paper marked with its name.*

Twelfth, I will *let each spot dry and repeat steps 8 and 9 until each spot is very dark. I can keep doing this for several days, if I cover the saucers with plastic wrap.*

Thirteenth, I will *tape each filter paper to a pencil and place the pencil across the rim of the jar or cup. If paper touches the bottom, I will cut some off the top and tape it again. The bottom edge of the paper should be about 1/4 inch from the bottom of the jar.*

Fourteenth, I will *take the paper out of the jar and pour about 1/4 inch of saltwater into the jar. Then I will carefully put the paper back into the jar. The saltwater should just touch the bottom of the paper but must not touch the color dots.*

Fifteenth, I will *let the saltwater creep up the paper until it almost reaches the pencil.*

Sixteenth, I will *take the paper out and use a pencil to carefully circle each color spot that has appeared.*

Seventeenth, I will *make a colored drawing of each paper because the spots on the paper will soon disappear. I can also ask an adult to take a color photograph of each paper.*

Eighteenth, I will *compare the spots made by the candies to the spots made by the dyes. Measure how far the yellow dye is from the starting line. If a spot made by a candy is the same distance from the starting line and is the same color as the spot made by the yellow dye, then the candy has yellow dye in it. Repeat this for each spot.*

Nineteenth, I will _need to use a table like the one_
below.
If you have a computer in your classroom or at home,
you may use it to make your data tables. Ask your teacher
or your parents to show you how.

DYE COLOR	RED M&M	BLUE M&M	GREEN M&M	YELLOW M&M	BROWN M&M
RED					
BLUE					
YELLOW					
GREEN					

For this Science Fair Project I will not have any other data tables and
I will not need graphs.

Other ideas I can try:
- I can try other colors of the candies.
- I can test other kinds of candy.
- I can try to get the food dyes that candy companies or bakeries use and test them.

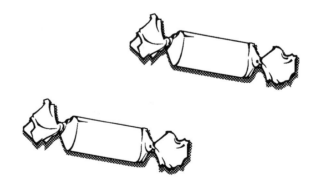

WORKSHEET 4
GETTING READY

Making your project a controlled experiment

To make my project a controlled experiment, I will do one of the following:

The one thing I will change is _____

_____

OR

I will count only the *colors that appear* _____
in one special place, *the filter paper strip.* _____

OR

I will measure _____
after a certain amount of time, _____

IF I HAVE TWO GROUPS IN MY SCIENCE FAIR PROJECT:
The group that I do something to is the Experimental Group.

My Experimental Group is _____

The group I do not do anything different to is the Control Group.

My Control Group is _____

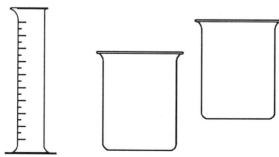

**WORKSHEET 5
UNDERSTANDING YOUR DATA**

Answer the following questions if they apply to your Science Fair Project. You will probably not use all the questions.

What new data tables do I need to make? *none.*

Did one thing happen the most? *I will tell the number of colors I find.*

Did one thing happen the least? *No.*

Would the average number help me? *No.*

Did one kind change more than the others? *No.*

Did all the things change in the same way? *No.*

Now write your observations below:

_____

_____

_____

Now you're on your own to complete your project —there's some help on the next pages, though!

You have made what scientists call a chromatogram. The color spots are from colored material (called a pigment) in the dye. You may be able to see several different color spots from one candy color. The companies that make the candies may use some dyes that are not the same as the ones you can buy in the grocery store. You can add the exact names of the dyes you tested to your data tables. The dyes from the store are yellow #5, red #40, blue #1, and red #3. Did you find several color spots from any of the dyes you used?

Here are some ideas for your display:
- use photographs of the chromatograms on your backboard,
- use the jars, empty candy bags, and food dyes as props,
- set up a new chromatogram in the jar as an example,
- put your chromatograms on your display.

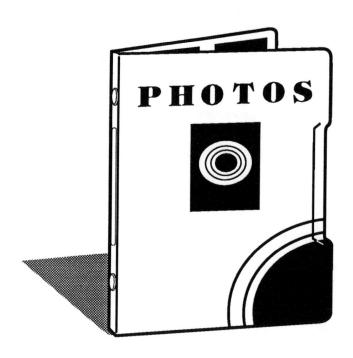

Project Ideas in Chemistry

1. How much calcium is in bones?

Use two chicken bones of about the same size. Any kind of bone that has been completely cleaned of meat will do. Try several different kinds of bones if you can. Place one of the bones in household vinegar and the other in water for two to three weeks. Vinegar will dissolve the calcium in the bone. You will be able to bend it. See if different bones become flexible in less time. Your control is the bone in water.

2. Can you tell if a piece of fabric or material is old?

You can tell if thread or material is old by how it looks in "black light." Black lights are ultraviolet lights that are sold in some stores; they make some posters glow.

NOTE: You will need adult supervision for this project. Ultraviolet light is harmful to your eyes.

Find some old clothes or thread and see if there is a difference in how it glows when compared to modern material. Washing material in modern detergents also makes it glow. Take pictures of the different materials in ultraviolet light.

3. Can you make dyes from plants?

Long ago people made their own dyes for clothing. You can make dyes from many fruits, flowers, and vegetables. Some good ones to try are beets, marigolds, mulberries, cabbage, onion skins, and walnut shells.

NOTE: You will need adult supervision for this project. Ask an adult to help you with the stove or hot plate.

Put about a cup of the plant material in a small pot with 2 cups of water. Boil the mixture for about 15 minutes, remove the pot from the heat, mash the mixture carefully with a potato masher, and strain the liquid into a bowl. Throw the mashed plant away and return the juice to the pot. Put the pot on low heat and use tongs to carefully add pieces of different kinds of white fabric (cotton, linen, wool, etc.). Compare the darkness of the dye on the different fabrics and the time it takes to get a certain color.

4. How are the "weights" of motor oil different?

Some motor oil is labeled 10 W 30 and some is 10 W 40. Different "weights" are recommended for different uses and different times of year. You can do an experiment to see the differences. Pour equal amounts of different motor oils into an old clear glass vase or large jar. Record the time it takes for a plastic bead to fall to the bottom. This will give you an idea of the oil's stickiness (viscosity).

5. Can you see the difference between lowfat milk and whole milk?

Pour milk into a saucer and put one drop of different food colors in each "corner." Add a drop of liquid detergent to the middle of the milk. The food coloring will now mix with the milk. The detergent lets the dyes mix with the milk better by getting some of the fat out of the way. Try milk with different fat contents (2%, 1%, skimmed, goat's milk, buttermilk, heavy cream). Record and photograph or sketch the results. Your control is the whole milk.

6. How fast do crystals grow?

You can make your own crystals from powdered sugar, salt, Epsom salts, or granulated sugar.

NOTE: You will need adult supervision for this project. Ask an adult to help you with the stove or hot plate.

Heat 2 cups of water on the stove until it is ready to boil, add sugar or salt until no more will dissolve in the water. Let the liquid cool a bit and pour it into a glass jar. Tie a paper clip to a piece of string or yarn. Hang the string from a pencil placed across the top of the jar. Find a place to put the jar so that it will not be moved. Crystals will begin to grow on the string in a few days. Compare how long it takes crystals of different kinds to grow. Compare their shapes.

7. How well do all stain removers work?

You can do your own commercial by testing how well different stain removers work. Use different types of fabrics, stain each one with a measured amount of grape juice or tomato sauce, and put one stain remover on each spot. Wash the pieces of fabric in exactly the same way and compare the results. Your control is the stain on each type of material without any stain remover. You can photograph the results.

8. How much vitamin C is in different fruit juices?

Crush a vitamin C tablet and dissolve it in distilled water. Mix one teaspoon of cornstarch in 1 cup of distilled water and add 3 drops of tincture of iodine. This should make the cornstarch solution blue. Pour 3 tablespoons of the blue liquid into a glass and count the number of drops of the vitamin C solution it takes to make the liquid turn clear. Test different juices to see how much vitamin C they have by following the same steps. Compare the number of drops of juice it takes to make the liquid clear. Your control is the number of drops of vitamin C solution.

9. How do detectives tell the difference in inks?

Can you find the difference between several blue felt tip pens? Cut a coffee filter into 1-inch strips and cut the bottom of each strip into a point. Measure the height of a glass or plastic jar and cut the strips 1 inch longer that the jar's height. Make a small dot 1 inch from the bottom of one strip of coffee filter with each pen. Put about 1/2 inch of water in the jar. Fold over 1 inch of the top of the first strip and hang it over a pencil placed over the top of the jar. The pointed tip of the strip should touch the water. After the water and ink have moved up the strip, remove it, and repeat the steps with another ink and strip.

10. Can you test the amount of the enzyme, diastase, present in seeds?

Seeds like barley or lima beans have food stored in them to help the new plant live until it can make its own food. As these seeds are sprouting (germinating), they make a chemical called an enzyme that lets them use the food stored in the seed. The enzyme is called diastase. Let barley or bean seeds start to sprout for 24 hours, crush the seeds, and collect the liquid. Find out about the iodine test for starch. You can use the iodine you buy to put on cuts. Make a starch solution with cornstarch. Add 5 drops of the diastase to one teaspoon of starch solution and test with iodine. Continue with more drops. You can expand your experiment by letting the seeds germinate longer, trying different kinds of seeds, and testing if heating the diastase changes the results.

Children's Literature about Chemistry

Aaseng, Nathan. *The Inventors: Nobel Prizes in Chemistry, Physics, and Medicine.* Lerner, 1988.

Alcock, Vivian. *The Monster Garden.* Bantam/Doubleday/Dell, 1988.

Busenberg, Bonnie. *Vanilla, Chocolate, and Strawberry: The Story of Your Favorite Flavors.* Lerner, 1994.

Ehlert, Lois. *Red Leaf, Yellow Leaf.* Harcourt Brace Jovanovich, 1991.

Fisher, Leonard Everett. *Marie Curie.* Macmillan, 1994.

Forsyth, Adrian. *How Monkeys Make Chocolate: Foods and Medicines from the Rainforests.* Firefly, 1995.

Gherman, Beverly. *The Mysterious Rays of Dr. Roentgen.* Atheneum, 1994.

Haines, Gail Kay. *Sugar Is Sweet...and So Are Lots of Other Things.* Macmillan, 1992.

Hare, Tony. *Polluting the Air.* Watts, 1992.

Maestro, Betsy. *Why Do Leaves Change Color.* HarperCollins, 1994.

Nottridge, Rhoda. *Additives.* Lerner, 1993.

Parker, Steve. *Marie Curie and Radium.* HarperCollins, 1992.

Peters, Lisa Westberg. *Meg and David Discover Treasure in the Air.* Holt, 1995.

Pflaum, Rosalynd. *Marie Curie and Her Daughter, Irene.* Lerner, 1993.

Silverstein, Alvin. *Vitamins and Minerals.* Millbrook, 1992.

Silverstein, Alvin. *Fats.* Millbrook, 1992.

Silverstein, Alvin. *Proteins.* Millbrook, 1992.

Vare, Ethlie Ann. *Adventurous Spirit: A Story about Ellen Swallow Richards.* Carolrhoda, 1992.

Westray, Kathleen. *A Color Sampler.* Ticknor & Fields, 1993.

CHAPTER 7

Sample Projects and Project Ideas on the Environment

This chapter (and each chapter in Part 3) contains two complete sample projects, a list of ideas for projects, and a list of children's literature about the chapter topic.

Each sample project has complete step-by-step instructions and answers for many of the worksheets. The child may use the answers provided and write them on his or her own worksheets. You and the student may have different answers that you want to use and may wish to modify the procedure.

The data gathering will be done by the student. Data tables are set up for ease of use and graph templates are provided. The student will need to complete the remainder of the worksheets and place them in the Experimental Notebook.

Additional ideas, props for the display, and resource books are suggested.

Sample Project #7

Idea: How do monuments become worn away?

Background: People often say that old statues in the park or old cemetery gravestones are being destroyed by acid rain and other pollution. These monuments are made of marble, but they are being worn away or eroded. You can find out how this happens by using small pieces of the marble or limestone and some vinegar.

Books to read about this project:
  an encyclopedia article on marble
  an encyclopedia article on limestone
  bibliography no. 18
  bibliography no. 35
  bibliography no. 50

WORKSHEET 1
PICKING YOUR PROJECT

What can you count or measure with your ideas?

Write below what you can count or measure for your ideas. Follow the examples I gave on what I could count or measure for my ideas.

1. For my idea # 1, I can count (or measure) _the change in the weight (or mass) of pieces of marble or limestone chips._

2. For my idea #2, I can count (or measure) _____

3. For my idea #3, I can count (or measure) _____

Which idea do you like best? Ask your parents or your teacher if they agree with you, then write the idea you chose on the lines below.

My idea for my Science Fair Project: _How do monuments become worn away?_

WORKSHEET 2
PLANNING YOUR PROJECT

Now let's see what you need to do to plan your
Science Fair Project.

Write your idea again. *How do monuments become worn away?*

Write what you will count or measure again. *I will measure the change in the weight (or mass) of pieces of marble or limestone.*

To plan my project:

First, I will need to READ *about marble and limestone and how it is worn away.*

Second, I will need *to find out where I can get some small pieces of marble or limestone.*

Third, I will need *to ask my parents for some old glass jars and some kitchen vinegar.*

Fourth, I will need *find a scale to weigh the pieces of marble or limestone (I can ask my teacher or maybe my parents have a postage or diet scale I can use).*

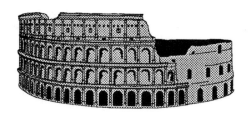

WORKSHEET 3
PLANNING TO GATHER YOUR DATA

Now let's see what you need to do to gather data on your Science Fair Project.

Write what you will count or measure. *I will measure* *the change in the weight (or mass) of pieces of* *marble or limestone.*

To plan to record my data:

First, I will *find where I can get the pieces of marble* *or limestone.*

NOTE: You can usually find one of these materials at landscaping or gravel companies. Marble chips can also be purchased from Science Kit and Boreal Laboratories in *Appendix B.*

Second, I will *get the old glass jars and label them.*

Third, I will *learn how to use the scale. I should* *weigh something that has a known weight (like a* *small candy bar that has the weight on the label). I* *will learn about the unit that the scale uses (grams* *or ounces).*

Fourth, I will *weigh each piece of the marble on the* *scale and put it in one of the labeled jars.*

Fifth, I will *need to use a table like the one on the* *next page.*

If you have a computer in your classroom or at home, you may use it to make your data tables. Ask your teacher or your parents to show you how.

PIECE	A	B	C	D	E	F	G	H	I	J
WEIGHT BEFORE (in grams)										
WEIGHT AFTER 1 WEEK (in grams)										
WEIGHT AFTER 2 WEEKS (in grams)										
WEIGHT AFTER 3 WEEKS (in grams)										
WEIGHT AFTER 4 WEEKS (in grams)										
WEIGHT AFTER 5 WEEKS (in grams)										

Sixth, I will *put enough water in jars A and B to cover the piece of marble or limestone.*

Seventh, I will *put enough vinegar in the remaining jars to cover the pieces of stone.*

Eighth, I will *cover each jar with plastic wrap.*

Ninth, I will *use tweezers or an old spoon to take each stone out of its jar and put it on paper towels to dry. I will weigh the piece and record the weight in my data table each week for each piece.*

Tenth, I will *check (every other day) that there is enough water in jars A and B and that there is enough vinegar in the other jars to cover the pieces.*

Other ideas I can try:
- I can take photographs of some of the monuments in my town.
- If I can find some old gravestones (from the 1700s or the1800s),
  I can measure their thickness at the top and at the bottom.
  Sometimes there a difference in the thickness because of
  erosion. If I can find a tool called a caliper, I will be able to
  measure the thickness better than with a ruler.

WORKSHEET 4
GETTING READY

Making your project a controlled experiment

To make my project a controlled experiment, I will do one
of the following:

The one thing I will change is _if the pieces of marble or
limestone are in water or in vinegar._

I will count only the _____
in one special place, _____

I will measure _____
after a certain amount of time, _____

IF I HAVE TWO GROUPS IN MY SCIENCE FAIR PROJECT:
The group that I do something to is the Experimental Group.

My Experimental Group is _the pieces of stone in vinegar._

The group I do not do anything different to is the Control
Group.

My Control Group is _the pieces of stone in water._

WORKSHEET 5
UNDERSTANDING YOUR DATA

Answer the following questions if they apply to your Science Fair Project. You will probably not use all the questions.

What new data tables do I need to make? *I will make a data table to compare the weights before with the final weights on the last week of my experiment.*

Did one thing happen the most? *I will tell whether the pieces in the vinegar or in the water changed in weight.*

Did one thing happen the least? *No.*

Would the average number help me? *No.*

Did one kind change more than the others? *No.*

Did all the things change in the same way? *No.*

Now write your observations below:

_____

_____

Now you're on your own to complete your project —there's some help on the next pages, though!

Now you will make your graphs. You can use the example below.

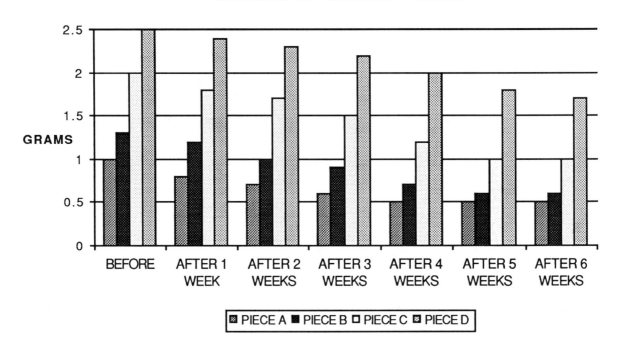

WEIGHTS OF MARBLE PIECES

PIECE A ⊠ PIECE B ■ PIECE C □ PIECE D ⊠

Here are some ideas for your display:
- use photographs of the monuments or statues in your town on your backboard,
- use the jars, the marble pieces, and the scale as props.

Sample Project #8

Idea: How long do different building materials hold heat?

Background: It always seems hotter when you are in a big city than when you are out in the countryside. Does the macadam of parking lots and the concrete and brick of buildings hold more heat than grass? You can find out!

Books to read about this project:
>   an encyclopedia article on heat and the environment
>   bibliography no. 19
>   bibliography no. 50
>   bibliography no. 63

WORKSHEET 1
PICKING YOUR PROJECT

What can you count or measure with your ideas?

Write below what you can count or measure for your ideas. Follow the examples I gave on what I could count or measure for my ideas.

1. For my idea # 1, I can count (or measure) *how long it takes different materials to lose heat.*

2. For my idea #2, I can count (or measure)_____

3. For my idea #3, I can count (or measure) _____

Which idea do you like best? Ask your parents or your teacher if they agree with you, then write the idea you chose on the lines below.

My idea for my Science Fair Project: *How long do different materials hold heat?*

WORKSHEET 2
PLANNING YOUR PROJECT

Now let's see what you need to do to plan your
Science Fair Project.

Write your idea again. *How long do different*
materials hold heat?

Write what you will count or measure again. *I will*
measure how long it takes different materials to
lose heat.

To plan my project:

First, I will need to READ *about heat, temperature,*
and how heat affects the environment.

Second, I will need *to find containers to put the*
different materials in (like 9-inch by 11-inch foil
baking dishes) and a thermometer.

Third, I will need *to ask my parents if I can use a*
heat lamp or a desk lamp with a neck that bends.

Fourth, I will need *to find bricks, concrete blocks, and*
grass that I can dig up or grass seed and potting
soil, and garden dirt or potting soil.

WORSHEET 3
PLANNING TO GATHER YOUR DATA

Now let's see what you need to do to gather data on your Science Fair Project.

Write what you will count or measure. *I will measure how long it takes different materials to lose heat.*

To plan to record my data:

First, I will *get the containers to put the materials in.*

Second, I will *get the different materials, the lamp, and the thermometer.*

Third, I will *put one material in the container and fasten the thermometer so that its bulb is one half inch above the surface of the material.*

Fourth, I will *need to use a table like the one below.*

If you have a computer in your classroom or at home, you may use it to make your data tables. Ask your teacher or your parents to show you how.

MATERIAL	TEMP. START	TEMP. AFTER 1 min.	TEMP. AFTER 2 min.	TEMP. AFTER 3 min.	TEMP. AFTER 4 min.
BRICK					
CONCRETE					
GRASS					
SOIL					
WATER					

Fifth, I will *place the lamp exactly 6 inches above the top of the material and shine the lamp on the material for exactly half an hour.*

Sixth, I will *immediately record the temperature on the thermometer after the half hour.*

Seventh, I will *record the temperature every minute for about 10 minutes or until the temperature reads the same for three readings in a row.*

Eighth, I will *follow these steps for each of the materials I want to test.*

Ninth, I will *run at least three trials for each material.*

Tenth, I will *be sure to shine the lamp on each material for exactly one half hour from exactly the same height.*

Other ideas I can try:
- I can take photographs of my experiment.
- I can try other materials like patching concrete or macadam that can be mixed in small amounts.
- I can make a map of places around my house that are covered with concrete or macadam and places that have grass.

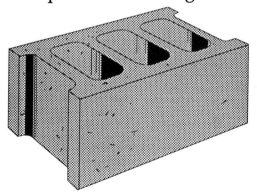

WORKSHEET 4
GETTING READY

Making your project a controlled experiment

To make my project a controlled experiment,
I will do one of the following:

The one thing I will change is _the kind of material._

I will count only the _____
in one special place, _____

I will measure _____
after a certain amount of time, _____

IF I HAVE TWO GROUPS IN MY SCIENCE FAIR PROJECT:
The group that I do something to is the Experimental Group.

My Experimental Group is _the different materials._

The group I do not do anything different to is the Control Group.

My Control Group is _the grass._

WORKSHEET 5
UNDERSTANDING YOUR DATA

Answer the following questions if they apply to your Science Fair Project. You will probably not use all the questions.

What new data tables do I need to make? *I will make a data table to show the number of degrees of temperature that each material lost.*

Did one thing happen the most? *I will tell whether the man-made materials or the natural materials lost the most heat.*

Did one thing happen the least? *I will tell whether the man-made materials or the natural materials lost the least heat.*

Would the average number help me? *Yes. The average of all the trials for each kind of material will help me understand my data.*

Did one kind change more than the others? *Yes.*

Did all the things change in the same way? *No.*

Now write your observations below:

_____

_____

_____

The other data table could look like this:

MATERIAL	TEMP. AFTER HEATING FOR 30 MIN.	TEMP. AFTER COOLING FOR 10 MIN.	DIFFERENCE IN TEMP.
BRICK			
CONCRETE			
GRASS			
DIRT			
WATER			

Now you will make your graphs. You can use the example below.

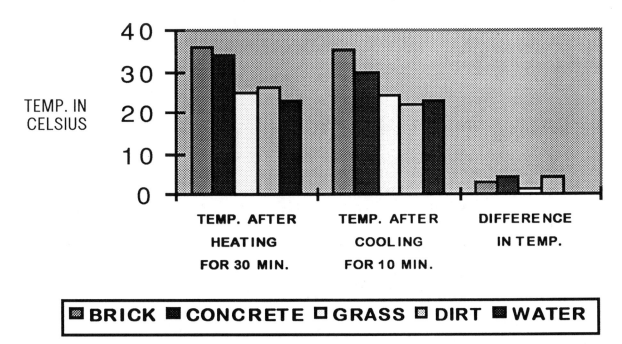

Here are some ideas for your display:
- use photographs of the monuments or statues in your town on your backboard,
- use the jars, the marble pieces, and the scale as props.

⌐ject Ideas on the Environment

1. Do all colors absorb the same amount of heat?

Use the same size piece of as many colors as possible of construction paper or poster board. Place them outdoors on snow on a sunny day. Be sure they are all in the sun. Record how far each color sinks into the snow after a certain amount of time.

2. Does acid rain affect car paint?

Paint pieces of aluminum or wood with car paint or find a small piece of a wrecked car at a junk yard and cut it into pieces. Save one piece for your "before" and one piece to put in distilled water for the control. Place the other pieces in vinegar and record changes. Before and after photographs would be helpful.

3. Do magnetic fields affect plant growth?

Make a weak electromagnetic field and grow houseplants inside it. Your control group is a set of plants growing in the same conditions but without an electromagnetic field.

4. Is there acid snow?

We have all heard of acid rain; but can snow be acidic, too? Gather samples of snow and test it with pH paper (special paper that measures how acidic something is. This is usually available at swimming pool supply stores or see Appendix B). Find out what the pH level is of the rain in your state or town and compare it to the pH of snow. Test distilled water for your control.

5. Does mold grow better in different colors of light?

Find out if bread mold grows faster in different colors of light, in daylight, or in the dark? Moisten pieces of bread (use bread without preservatives, if possible), place them on a clean counter for two hours, and then seal them in individual plastic bags. You will need two pieces of bread for the experimental group for each kind of light environment you are going to test and two pieces for your control group. Place the control bread in the bags on the counter; place some experimental groups (in the bags) under different colors of light, in the dark, and in the other environments you are testing. Different colors of light can come from colored light bulbs or from making a color filter for a white light bulb by pasting colored cellophane plastic into a cardboard frame. Record how long it takes for mold to grow and how much mold grows on each piece of bread.

NOTE: Be sure to NEVER open the plastic bags once they have been sealed because mold spores could make you sick.

6. How do stalagmites and stalactites grow?

You can grow your own stalagmites and stalactites with very simple supplies. Dissolve 2/3 cup of Epsom salts (magnesium sulfate) in 1 cup of hot tap water and pour half into each of two glasses. Tie a paper clip to each end of a 12-inch piece of yarn or cotton string. Put one paper-clip end in each of the glasses and move the glasses so that the yarn droops a little in the middle. Place a saucer under the drooping middle of the yarn. The liquid will move through the yarn and begin to drip down the drooping center. It will form crystals as it drips and will make both a stalagmite and stalactite. Record how long it takes for stalagmites and stalactites to grow. You can experiment with different amounts of Epsom salts and different room temperatures.

7. How much water can you collect by condensation?

The water cycle on Earth happens because of evaporation (water turning into gas and making clouds) and condensation (rain, snow, frost, and dew). Wind and temperature make the water cycle happen at different speeds. Place a small dish inside a bigger dish. Put a measured amount of water in the large dish and cover the top with plastic wrap. Put a small weight (a marble or a washer) in the middle of the plastic wrap to make it sink down a little in the middle. Carefully put the dishes in the sun. Record how much water drips off the inside of the plastic wrap and into the small dish. Test different temperatures. Does your miniature water cycle work better if you put it where it is hot in the daytime and move it to the refrigerator at night?

8. How can you make seeds sprout faster?

Some seeds need to wait over the winter in order to sprout; some seeds need light to make them sprout; and some seeds will sprout faster if soaked in water over night. You can make a helpful chart for gardeners by testing what things make certain seeds germinate (or sprout) faster. Find out what seeds your family, friends or neighbors like to plant. Buy packages of these seeds and try to germinate them in different conditions. Put about 10 seeds between moist layers of paper towels on a dish. Check each day to see how many seeds sprouted and be sure to keep the paper towels damp. You can test each type of seed in different temperatures, in light or dark, soaked for 24 hours or kept in the freezer for several weeks. Compare the number or percent of seeds that sprout in each environment. Your control group will be the seeds at room temperature.

9. How much salt can you remove by evaporation?

Taking salt out of sea water to make it drinkable (desalination) is important to many places that do not have enough fresh drinking water. You can see how much salt you can take out of salt water by evaporation. Mix a measured amount of salt with 1 cup of distilled water. Pour it into a large flat pan (a cookie sheet with sides is a good choice) and wait until all the water evaporates. Carefully scrape out all of the salt left in the pan and measure the amount. Is it the same as when you started? Try different amounts of salt. You can also experiment with different conditions for evaporation and time how long it takes all of the water to evaporate.

10. Do plastic bags break down?

Everyone is worried about our garbage dumps and landfills because we all throw away so much trash. We recycle many things. We use many plastic bags — for sandwiches, to store things, and for packaging. Do they ever break down, or decompose? You can find out! Put labels on 10 plastic sandwich bags and place two of them in a drawer for your control group. Place two more in sunlight, two in the freezer, and two outside where they won't blow away. Bury two sandwich bags or put them under the dirt in a bucket or large flower pot that you can leave outside. After three weeks, gather all the bags and fill them with water. See if they leak.

Children's Literature about the Environment

Accorsi, William. *Rachel Carson.* Holiday House, 1993.

Aliki. *Fossils Tell of Long Ago.* Thomas Y. Crowell, 1990.

Aliki. *My Visit to the Aquarium.* HarperCollins, 1993.

Asch, Frank. *Water.* Harcourt Brace, 1995.

Baker, Jeannie. *Where the Forest Meets the Sea.* Greenwillow, 1988.

Brown, Ruth. *The World That Jack Built.* Dutton Children's Books, 1991.

Cech, John. *First Snow, Magic Snow.* FourWinds, 1992.

Cherry, Lynne. *The Great Kapok Tree: A Tale of the Amazon Rain Forest.* Harcourt Brace Jovanovich, 1990.

Cole, Joanna. *The Magic School Bus at the Waterworks.* Scholastic, 1986.

Conover, Chris. *Sam Panda and Thunder Dragon.* Farrar, Straus and Giroux, 1992.

Dunphy, Madeleine. *Here is the Tropical Rain Forest.* Hyperion Books for Children, 1994.

George, Jean Craighead. *The Missing 'Gator of Gumbo Limbo: An Ecological Mystery.* HarperCollins, 1992.

George, Jean Craighead. *One Day in the Tropical Rain Forest.* Thomas Y. Crowell, 1990.

George, Jean Craighead. *Who Really Killed Cock Robin?: An Ecological Mystery.* HarperCollins, 1991.

Ketterman, Helen. *The Year of No More Corn.* Orchard Books, 1993.

Killion, Bette. *The Same Wind.* HarperCollins, 1992.

Leedy, Loreen. *The Great Trash Bash.* Holiday House, 1991.

Markle, Sandra. *A Rainy Day.* Orchard, 1993.

Ransom, Candice F. *Listening to Crickets: A Story about Rachel Carson.* Lerner, 1993.

Silver, Donald. *One Small Square: Backyard.* W. H. Freeman, 1993.

Turner, Ann. *A Moon for Seasons.* Macmillan, 1994.

Weeks, Sarah. *Hurricane City.* HarperCollins, 1993.

Whittington, Mary K. *Winter's Child.* Atheneum, 1992.

CHAPTER 8

Sample Projects and Project Ideas with Microscopes

This chapter (and each chapter in Part 3) contains two complete sample projects, a list of ideas for projects, and a list of children's literature about the chapter topic.

Each sample project has complete step-by-step instructions and answers for many of the worksheets. The child may use the answers provided and write them on his or her own worksheets. You and the student may have different answers that you want to use and may wish to modify the procedure.

The data gathering will be done by the student. Data tables are set up for ease of use and graph templates are provided. The student will need to complete the remainder of the worksheets and place them in the Experimental Notebook.

Additional ideas, props for the display, and resource books are suggested.

Before you begin to read about these microscope projects, you will need to know some things about microscopes and magnifying glasses. For most microscope projects you should have a compound microscope or a stereomicroscope. These kinds are pictured on the next page. It may be

157

possible to borrow one from a school. A compound microscope usually magnifies an object 40, 100, or 400 times. The books you will read about microscopes will explain how to figure out the magnification of different microscopes. Stereomicroscopes generally magnify only 2 or 4 times. Some microscope projects can be done with a magnifying glass or with a hand-held, inexpensive microscope that is sold in some electronics stores and catalogs (Appendix B). Magnifying glasses can magnify 2 to 10 times and hand-held microscopes usually magnify 30 times. Magnification is shown by an "x". For example, a magnification of 100 times is written 100x.

The sample projects and project ideas in this chapter are marked with symbols to tell you which kind of microscope or magnifier will be needed. The symbols are shown next to the diagrams on the different kinds of microscopes below.

Compound Microscope
(Symbol: CM)

Stereomicroscope
(Symbol: SM)

Hand-held Microscope
(Symbol: HM)

Magnifying Glass
(Symbol: MG)

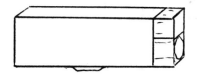

Sample Project #9   (HM, SM, or CM)

Idea: Does every grain of sand look the same?

Background: You have probably seen lots of sand at the beach or in a sandbox. Did you ever look at just one grain of sand? Does every grain look the same? There are really many kinds of sand. You can get samples of sand from different places and look at them with a microscope. Ask your friends or relatives to bring you some sand from their vacation or from where they live.

Books to read about this project:
  an encyclopedia article on sand
  a book on how to use a microscope
  bibliography no. 11
  bibliography no. 49
  bibliography no. 50
  bibliography no. 61

WORKSHEET 1
PICKING YOUR PROJECT

What can you count or measure with your ideas?

Write below what you can count or measure for your ideas.
Follow the examples I gave on what I could count or
measure for my ideas.

1. For my idea # 1, I can count (or measure) *the
different kinds of sand grains and measure the
sizes of the sand grains.*

2. For my idea #2, I can count (or measure) _____

_____

3. For my idea #3, I can count (or measure) _____

_____

Which idea do you like best? Ask your parents or your
teacher if they agree with you, then write the idea you
chose on the lines below.

My idea for my Science Fair Project: *Does every grain
of sand look the same?*

WORKSHEET 2
PLANNING YOUR PROJECT

Now let's see what you need to do to plan your Science Fair Project.

Write your idea again. _Does every grain of sand look the same?_

Write what you will count or measure again. _I will count the different kinds of sand grains and measure the sizes._

To plan my project:

First, I will need to READ _about sand and microscopes._

Second, I will need _to find different kinds of sand._

Third, I will need _to find a microscope and microscope slides._

Fourth, I will need _to learn how to use the microscope._

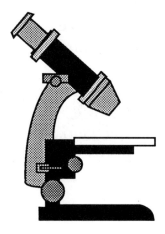

WORKSHEET 3
PLANNING TO GATHER YOUR DATA

Now let's see what you need to do to gather data on
your Science Fair Project.

Write what you will count or measure. *I will count the*
different kinds of sand grains and measure the sizes
of the grains of sand.

To plan to record my data:

First, I will *get different kinds of sand.*

Second, I will *put several grains of one type of sand*
on a microscope slide.

Third, I will *place the slide on the microscope stage*
and turn the lens selector to the lowest power.
NOTE: You can use any kind of microscope with any
magnification power for this Science Fair Project, but a
magnification of 20 or 30 is the best.

Fourth, I will *look at the slide with the other lenses*
on the microscope.

Note: If I have a compound microscope, I will
follow steps 5 and 6 below and then continue with
step 9 to the end. If I have a stereomicroscope, I
will skip steps 5 and 6 and continue with step 7 to
the end.

Fifth, I will *need to find a small, clear, plastic metric*
ruler with millimeter marks to use with the 10x,
20x, 40x, or 100x lenses of a compound microscope.

Sixth, I will *tape the ruler to the microscope slide to use with a compound microscope. I will place the ruler and slide on the microscope stage so that one of the millimeter marks is at the edge of the field of view.*

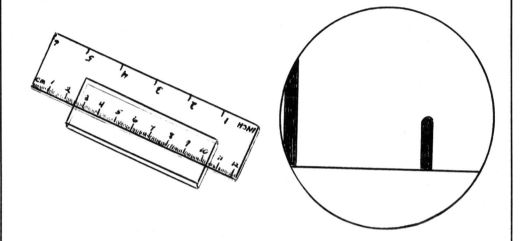

Seventh, I will *need to find graph paper with squares of 1/10 inch or 1 mm or 2 mm to use if I have a stereomicroscope.*

Eighth, I will *place the graph paper on the stage of the stereomicroscope and put the slide on top of the graph paper.*

Ninth, I will *use a small plate or glass to trace circles on plain paper (the circles should be about 3 inches across).*

Tenth, I will *use these circles to represent the view I have when I look through the microscope (the field of view).*

Eleventh, I will _make a drawing of one or two grains_ _of sand from the view I see with the magnification_ _that gives the sharpest image. I will try to make the_ _drawing "to scale." I will use the ruler or the graph_ _paper grid to help me draw the right size._

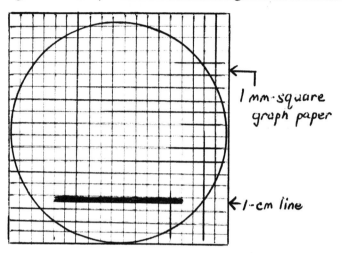

1 mm·square graph paper

← 1·cm line

Twelfth, I will _make a drawing of each different kind_ _of sand and I will use the same magnification for_ _each sample._

Thirteenth, I will _need to use tables like the one_ _below and the one on the next page._
If you have a computer in your classroom or at home, you may use it to make your data tables. Ask your teacher or your parents to show you how.

SAND SAMPLE	SIZE OF 1st GRAIN in mm	SIZE OF 2nd GRAIN in mm	SIZE OF 3rd GRAIN in mm	AVERAGE SIZE OF GRAINS in mm
A				
B				
C				
D				
E				

SAND SAMPLE	SHAPE	COLOR	TRANSPARENCY
A			
B			
C			
D			
E			

Fourteenth, I will _record the size of several grains of each different kind of sand. I will try to use grains that all seem to be of the same kind (sometimes samples of sand are mixtures of many kinds of different particles. I can do something a little different with these kinds of sands — see step 16)._

Fifteenth, I will _describe the shape, color, and transparency of the grains of each sample._

Sixteenth, I will _do something different with samples of sand that have a variety of particles in them. I will put about 30 grains into a field of view and record the exact number. Then I will record the number of grains of each kind (look at the table on the next page) . I will use the same magnification for each sample._

NUMBER OF DIFFERENT PARTICLES

SAND SAMPLE	SHELL PIECES	VOLCANIC MATERIAL	QUARTZ	COLORED MINERALS
A				
B				
C				
D				
E				

Seventeenth, I will _use the books on sand to try to tell which type of sand each kind is._

Other ideas I can try:
- If I can find a camera to fit on the microscope, I can take photographs of the different kinds of sand.
- If I have a penpal or friends or family in other states, I can ask them to send me some sand.
- I can graph the percentage of different kinds of particles in my samples (shell fragments, volcanic material, quartz, etc.).
- I can weigh a certain volume of each kind of sand to find the density.
- I can try to dissolve some of the sand in vinegar.

WORKSHEET 4
GETTING READY

Making your project a controlled experiment

To make my project a controlled experiment, I will do one of the following:

The one thing I will change is *the kind of sand, not the magnification.* _____

I will count only the _____
in one special place, _____

I will measure _____
after a certain amount of time, _____

IF I HAVE TWO GROUPS IN MY SCIENCE FAIR PROJECT:
The group that I do something to is the Experimental Group.

My Experimental Group is _____
The group I do not do anything different to is the Control Group.
My Control Group is _____

WORKSHEET 5
UNDERSTANDING YOUR DATA

Answer the following questions if they apply to your Science Fair Project. You will probably not use all the questions.

What new data tables do I need to make? *None.*

Did one thing happen the most? *I will tell the average size of each kind of sand.*

Did one thing happen the least? *No.*

Would the average number help me? *I have the average size already.*

Did one kind change more than the others? *No.*

Did all the things change in the same way? *No.*

Now write your observations below:

_____

_____

_____

Now you're on your own to complete your project —there's some help on the next pages, though!

Now you will make your graphs. You can use the example below.

SIZE OF SAND GRAINS (in mm)

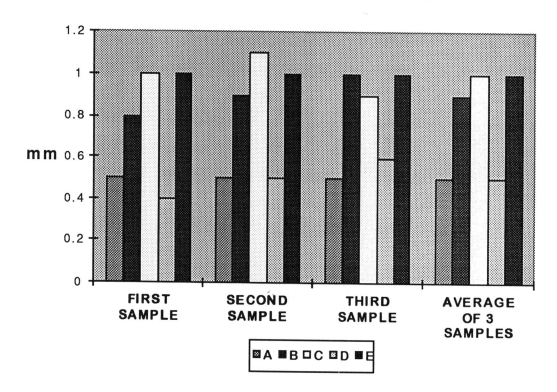

COMPOSITION OF SAND

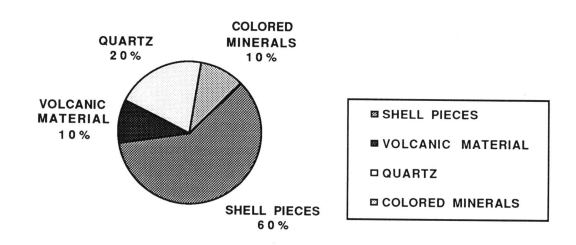

Here are some ideas for your display:
- use your drawings or photographs of the grains of sand on your backboard,
- mount samples of each kind of sand on colored poster board to use as props,
- use clear glue to attach some grains of each type of sand to labeled microscope slides and have the slides and the microscope on your table for the people to see.

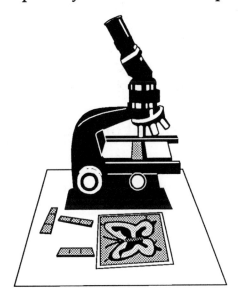

Sample Project #10   (CM, SM, HM, or MG)

Idea: Can you find meteorites in your own backyard?

Background: Since the earth was formed, many millions of meteorites have fallen onto the earth. Some are huge; the largest ever reported weigh 60 tons. Some are very tiny, only one millimeter in diameter. The small ones are called micrometeorites and you may be able to find some around your house. All meteorites contain metal; most earth rocks do not. If you have a microscope, a magnet, and a rain gutter on the edge of your roof that your parents can reach safely, you can look for micrometeorites!

Books to read about this project:
      an encyclopedia article on meteorites
      a book on how to use a microscope
      bibliography no. 11
      bibliography no. 49
      bibliography no. 50
      bibliography no. 61
      bibliography no. 62

WORKSHEET 1
PICKING YOUR PROJECT

What can you count or measure with your ideas?

Write below what you can count or measure for your ideas.
Follow the examples I gave on what I could count or
measure for my ideas.

1. For my idea # 1, I can count (or measure) *I will count
the different meteorites and measure the sizes.*

2. For my idea #2, I can count (or measure)_____

Which idea do you like best? Ask your parents or your
teacher if they agree with you, then write the idea you
chose on the lines below.

My idea for my Science Fair Project: *Can you find
meteorites in your own backyard?*

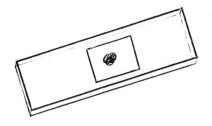

WORKSHEET 2
PLANNING YOUR PROJECT

Now let's see what you need to do to plan your
Science Fair Project.

Write your idea again. *Can you find meteorites in*
your own backyard?

Write what you will count or measure again. *I will count*
the different meteorites and measure the sizes.

To plan my project:

First, I will need to READ *about meteorites and*
microscopes.

Second, I will need *to ask my parents if they can*
safely reach the rain gutters of our house.

Third, I will need *to find a microscope, microscope*
slides, and a small magnet.

Fourth, I will need *to learn to use the microscope.*

WORKSHEET 3
PLANNING TO GATHER YOUR DATA

Now let's see what you need to do to gather data on
your Science Fair Project.

Write what you will count or measure. *I will count the*
different meteorites and measure the sizes.

To plan to record my data:

First, I will *ask my parents to get about one quarter*
cup of particles from the rain gutter.

Second, I will *drag the magnet through the particles*
in the sample my parents got from the rain gutter
and put the particles that stick to the magnet in a
plastic sandwich bag labeled "Magnetic."

Third, I will *put some of the particles that did not*
stick to the magnet in another plastic sandwich bag
labeled "Nonmagnetic."

Fourth, I will *put several of the magnetic particles on*
a microscope.

Fifth, I will *place the slide on the microscope stage*
and turn the lens selector to the lowest power.

NOTE: You can use any kind of microscope with any
magnification power for this Science Fair Project.

Sixth, I will *look at the slide with the other lenses*
on the microscope.

Note: If I have a compound microscope, I will follow steps 7 and 8 below and then continue with step 11 to the end. If I have a stereomicroscope, I will skip steps 7 and 8 and continue with step 9 to the end.

Seventh, I will *need to find a small, clear, plastic metric ruler with millimeter marks to use with the 10x, 20x, 40x, or 100x lenses of a compound microscope.*

Eighth, I will *tape the ruler to the microscope slide to use with a compound microscope. I will place the ruler and slide on the microscope stage so that one of the millimeter marks is at the edge of the field of view.*

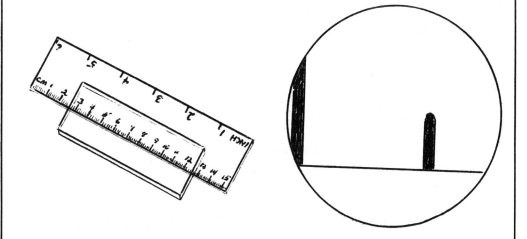

Ninth, I will *need to find graph paper with squares of 1/10 inch or 1 mm or 2 mm to use if I have a stereomicroscope.*

Tenth, I will *place the graph paper on the stage of the stereomicroscope and put the slide on top of the graph paper.*

Eleventh, I will *use a small plate or glass to trace circles on plain paper (the circles should be about 3 inches across).*

Twelfth, I will *use these circles to represent the view I have when I look through the microscope (the field of view).*

Thirteenth, I will *make a drawing of one or two of the meteorites from the view I see with the magnification that gives the sharpest image. I will try to make the drawing "to scale." I will use the ruler or the graph paper grid to help me draw the right size.*

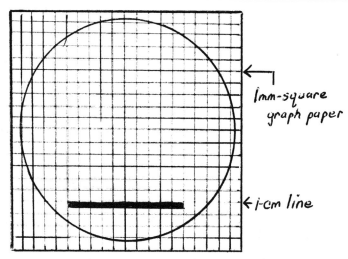

Fourteenth, I will *make a drawing of each different meteorite and I will use the same magnification for each sample.*

Fifteenth, I will *need to use tables like the ones on the next page.*

If you have a computer in your classroom or at home, you may use it to make your data tables. Ask your teacher or your parents to show you how.

METEORITE SAMPLE	SIZE in mm	COLOR	SHAPE	RUSTY	STONY
A					
B					
C					
D					
E					
F					
G					
H					

Sixteenth, I will _describe the color and shape of each meteorite._

Seventeenth, I will _make a check mark in the "Rusty" column if the meteorite has rust spots. Often the iron in a meteorite will become rusty if it is outside for a time._

Eighteenth, I will _make a check mark in the "Stony" column if the meteorite looks mostly like a stone._

Nineteenth, I will _follow the same steps and look at the particles from the rain gutter that were not magnetic._

Other ideas I can try:
- If I can find a camera to fit on the microscope, I can take photographs of the meteorites.
- If I have a penpal or friends or family in other states, I can ask them to send me some of the magnetic material from their rain gutters. NOTE: if they are children, they will have to ask their parents to get the samples for me.
- I can weigh a certain volume of the magnetic material from the rain gutters to find the density and compare this with the density of the nonmagnetic particles from the rain gutter.
- I can ask my parents to get samples every other week to see if there are any new meteorites.
- I can try to make new meteorites rust by putting them in a dish of water for a week. I can try this for meteorites that do not show any rust, too.

WORKSHEET 4
GETTING READY

Making your project a controlled experiment

To make my project a controlled experiment,
I will do one of the following:

The one thing I will change is _____

_____

OR

I will count only the *magnetic particles* _____
in one special place, _____

OR

I will measure _____
after a certain amount of time, _____

IF I HAVE TWO GROUPS IN MY SCIENCE FAIR PROJECT:
The group that I do something to is the Experimental Group.

My Experimental Group is *the meteorites (magnetic).*

The group I do not do anything different to is the Control
Group.

My Control Group is *the nonmagnetic particles from*
the rain gutter.

N   S

WORKSHEET 5
UNDERSTANDING YOUR DATA

Answer the following questions if they apply to your Science Fair Project. You will probably not use all the questions.

What new data tables do I need to make? _None._

Did one thing happen the most? _I will tell if most of the meteorites are rusty or stony or if they are of one color or shape._

Did one thing happen the least? _I will tell if one of the characteristics is the least common._

Would the average number help me? _The average size would help._

Did one kind change more than the others? _No._

Did all the things change in the same way? _No._

Now write your observations below:

_____

_____

_____

Now you're on your own to complete your project —there's some help on the next pages, though!

Now you will make your graphs. You can use the example below.

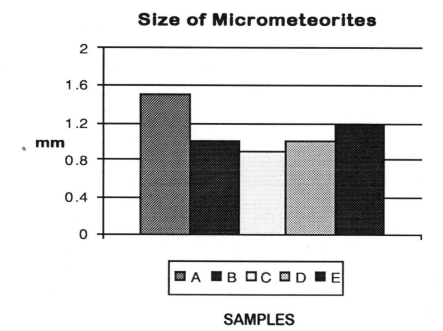

Size of Micrometeorites

mm

A B C D E

SAMPLES

Here are some ideas for your display:
- use your drawings or photographs of the micrometeorites on your backboard,
- use clear glue to mount each micrometeorite to microscope slides to use as props with your microscope. Label each one with the descriptive information you have found.

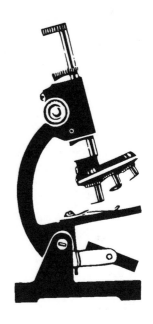

Project Ideas with Microscopes

1. Can you tell the difference between crystals? (CM, SM, HM, or MG)
Use a microscope to look at many different crystals. You can look at salt, sugar, colored sugar, MSG, alum, and Epsom salts. Ask you parents to see if the high school will give you a little bit of copper sulfate or other crystals. Draw or take photographs of the crystals.

2. Do all leaves have the same "breathing holes"? (CM)
Plants need to get air into their cells in order to live. They need carbon dioxide and oxygen. There are small "breathing holes," called stomates, in the surface of a leaf. You can see them quite clearly by carefully peeling off the underside of a leaf. Some plants have stomates only on the underside of their leaves (Norway maple); some have stomates on both sides (sunflower). You can make an interesting table to show which plants have stomates on which leaf surfaces.

3. Can you watch a population of microorganisms grow? (CM)
Yeast are microscopic organisms that we use to make bread and other things. Since they are so small, you can watch what happens to a whole "world" of them much easier than trying to watch a population of elephants. You can see how different foods or different temperatures make them grow faster or slower. Use 1 teaspoon of yeast from the package that you can buy at the grocery store. Put the yeast in a small jar with 1/2 cup warm water and 1/2 teaspoon of sugar. Stir the mixture well and place a drop on a microscope slide. Record the number of yeast cells you find in five different fields of view (see Sample Project 9 or 10) in a data table and figure the average number. Count and record the number of yeast cells everyday for about ten days. Follow these steps with another food, such as molasses or brown sugar, or keep the yeast in different temperatures.

4. Do fingerprints of family members look alike? (MG)
Most people know that each person has different fingerprints, but do people in the same family have fingerprints that have certain patterns that are alike? Use an ink pad or make a heavy layer of pencil marks on paper and roll your fingertip back and forth several times. Make your fingerprint on a plain white piece of paper by carefully rolling your fingertip from side to side just once. Use a magnifying glass to look at the pattern. Draw the

patterns you see and try to find things that are alike. Compare your fingerprint to those of other people in your family and to those of friends. You can try to find fingerprints on furniture or doorknobs. Use a little bit of baby powder (on dark surfaces) or graphite (on light surfaces). Place a piece of clear sticky tape over the fingerprint and carefully lift the tape. Stick the tape on dark or light paper and compare it to the fingerprints of your family.

5. Do bird feathers look alike? (CM, SM, HM, or MG)
Use feathers from pet birds and feathers that you find outside to see if they look alike under the microscope. Be sure to wash your hands after handling the feathers and throw the feathers away in a plastic bag as soon as you have looked at them. Sometimes there are bugs and germs on bird feathers. Draw the patterns you see and try to find things that are alike. Compare how the colors look when they are magnified.

6. Can you tell the difference between different clothing fibers? (CM)
Detectives use microscopes to find out about different kinds of clothing. Does cotton look like wool? Place a small piece of cotton thread, polyester thread, and yarn of different kinds on a slide. Draw or photograph what you see when you look at the fibers with the microscope. You can also look at how fabrics are woven.

7. Can you tell one person's hair from another's? (CM)
Ask for a sample of hair from your family, friends, and teachers. Try to get same hair from someone who has gray hair and from someone who bleaches or colors their hair, too. Draw or photograph the hairs under the microscope. Look for structures inside the hair and for the thickness and outside surface. You can also look at your pets' hair. Animal "fur" is really hair; wool is the hair of sheep. See if you can identify an unknown hair.

8. Can you see air pollution? (CM, SM, HM, or MG)
Sometimes you notice that certain places in your city or town seem to have more air pollution. Sometimes you can smell it; sometimes you can see it. Put a thin coat of petroleum jelly or some other clear sticky material on several microscope slides. Ask an adult to help you place slides where you think there is a lot of pollution. You can try to put your slides near

construction sites, near a busy street, or in an underground parking garage. Be sure to put the slides where they won't have dirt and dust from the ground blow onto them. You want to get samples of pollution that is in the air. Leave the slides at the sites for a day or two. Look at the slides with your microscope or magnifying glass. Make drawings or take photographs and make lists of the kinds of particles you find.

9. Is the pollen from all plants alike? (CM)

Many people have allergies to plant pollen. You can look at the differences between pollen from many kinds of plants. Put a drop of water on a slide and hold it under the stamen of a plant. Gently shake the plant so that some of the pollen falls onto the slide. Label the slide with the name of the plant and make a drawing of the pollen. Some pollen grains have microscopic wings or hooks.

10. Can you see blood moving in an animal? (CM)

Wouldn't it be interesting to see the blood moving through an animal's veins? You can, if you ask your parents to borrow a goldfish from your own aquarium or from a friend's. The fish will not be hurt at all. Carefully wrap the fish in paper towels that have been soaked with water. Leave the tail unwrapped and put the fish on a small, flat plate. Gently lay a microscope slide on top of the tail. Under the microscope you will be able to see blood moving (circulating) in the blood vessels of the tail.

Children's Literature about the Microscopic World

Aronson, Billy. *They Came from DNA.* W. H. Freeman, 1993.

Burns, Virginia Law. *Gentle Hunter: Biography of Alice Evans.* Enterprise, 1993.

Cobb, Vikki. *Natural Wonders: Stories Science Photos Tell.* Lothrop Lee & Shepard, 1990.

Cole, Joanna. *The Magic School Bus: Inside the Human Body.* Scholastic, 1989.

Cole, Joanna. *Your Insides.* Putnam, 1992.

Kaufman, Les. *Alligators to Zooplankton: A Dictionary of Water Babies.* Watts, 1991.

Lamboutne, Mike. *Inside Story.* Millbrook, 1992.

Lauber, Patricia. *What Do You See & How Do You See It?* Crown, 1994.

Lerner, Carol. *Plants That Make You Sniffle and Sneeze.* Morrow, 1993.

Maki, Chu. *Snowflakes, Sugar, and Salt: Crystals Up Close.* Lerner, 1993.

Markle, Sandra. *Outside and Inside You.* Macmillan, 1991.

Morgan, Nina. *Louis Pasteur.* Watts, 1992.

Parker, Steve. *The Body Atlas.* Dorling Kindersley, 1993.

Ruiz, Andres Llamas. *Animals on the Inside: A Book of Discovery & Learning.* Sterling, 1995.

Silver, Donald. *One Small Square: Cave.* W. H. Freeman, 1993.

Silver, Donald. *One Small Square: Seashore.* W. H. Freeman, 1993.

Taylor, Barbara. *Pond Life.* Dorling Kindersley, 1992.

Taylor, Kim. *Structure.* Wiley, 1992.

Tesar, Jenny. *Fungi.* Blackbirch, 1994.

Tesar, Jenny. *Microorganisms.* Blackbirch, 1994.

Verheyden-Hilliard, Mary Ellen. *Scientist and Physician, Judith Pachciary.* Equity Institute, 1988.

Wells, Robert E. *Is a Blue Whale the Biggest Thing There Is?* Albert Whitman, 1993.

Wells, Robert E. *What's Smaller Than a Pygmy Shrew?* Albert Whitman, 1993.

Wood, A. J. *Look Again! The Second Ultimate Spot-the-Difference Book.* Dial, 1992.

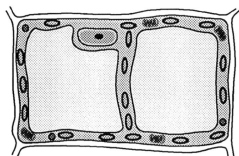

PART 4

SETTING UP A SCIENCE FAIR

CHAPTER 9

Easier than You Think

If your school does not have a science fair, someone (probably you, because you are interested enough to read this book) will have to get one started. At first thought the idea may seem daunting, but it can actually be quite simple. Teachers and parents who have been involved in setting up science fairs in their schools generally agree that what is required is someone who possesses good organizational skills and who is willing to do some serious pre-planning.

This chapter breaks the process down into manageable parts: decisions to make about what you want your science fair to be and easy steps to take to accomplish those parameters. Chapter 10 provides additional helpful hints, a checklist, and all kinds of reproducible paperwork ideas.

Decisions to make:
- Decision 1: How many participants?
- Decision 2: How many tables?
- Decision 3: How much space?
- Decision 4: When and where?
- Decision 5: Judging?
- Decision 6: Programs?

Decision 1: How many participants?

You may know the how many students are expected to participate or you may have to poll the various teachers involved. Your school may choose to begin with just one grade and build participation each year. You may even discover that only one teacher is ready to take up the challenge at the beginning. Do not be discouraged. Many quality science fair programs have begun with only one teacher's class. In this case, each year you will find that more and more teachers and classes will become involved.

Decision 2: How many tables?

You will need approximately 3 linear feet of table space for each participant. The common 6-foot school table will accommodate two projects. Multiply the number of participants you anticipate having by 2 to determine the number of tables you will need.

The availability of tables will influence many of the other decisions you will be making. Talk to the head custodian about what tables can be moved and a total number. Do not take "No" for an answer. If you meet with resistance, enlist the help of the Parent's Association, the director of the high school or middle school science fair, or an enthusiastic science teacher or administrator.

Decision 3: How much space?

Once the number of participants and the number of tables have been established, you will have to decide how much space you will need. Measure the length and width of the possible locations (cafeteria, all-purpose room, gymnasium, lobby area). Multiply the length and width of each room to determine the number of square feet.

While these simple formulas:

> Lobby Area: # of projects x 16 square feet
> Other Rooms: # of projects x 50 square feet

will give "ball park" figures, it would be wise to use the diagram on the next page to finalize the size requirements. Copy the next page, cut out the table diagrams, and try out several set-up plans. You can use some of the examples given on the following page. Be sure to allow adequate space for aisles between the tables. If you make the decision to have a judging session in which the students will participate, you will need wider aisles to accommodate chairs for the children.

1 square equals 2 feet   room size: 60 feet x 60 feet   table size: 2.5 feet x 6 feet

Here are two examples of how tables can be arranged in a room.

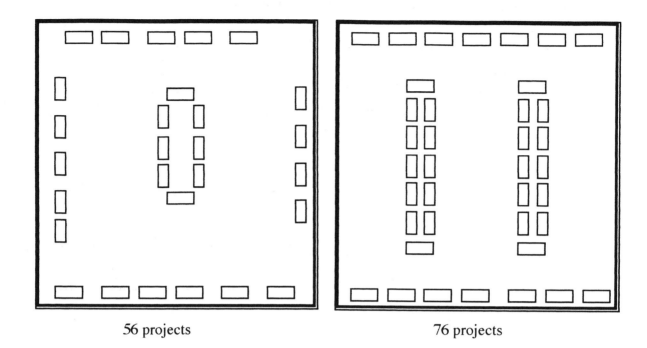

56 projects   76 projects

Decision 4: When and where?

The decisions of when and where to hold the science fair are interdependent. If you hold the science fair in the evening or on the weekend, you can investigate the possibility of using the cafeteria, the all-purpose room, the gymnasium, or the lobby area. If you want to hold the science fair during the school day, you may be limited to corridors or you may have to persuade administrators to reschedule regular uses of the gymnasium or the all-purpose room.

In the latter case, discuss the possibility of shifting the regularly scheduled uses with teachers and develop several solutions before speaking to the administrators. For example, suppose that you have decided to have the science fair on Wednesday during the school day and that the all-purpose room will be ideal. If the music teacher generally uses that room for choir practice on Mondays, Wednesdays, and Fridays, discuss the option of holding the rehearsal in one of the other rooms for that Wednesday. If you can arrange the switch with the music teacher, you will be in a better negotiating position when you speak to the administrators. When practical solutions with the support of those who will be most inconvenienced by them are offered, you will encounter less resistance. It is also wise to determine the table situation prior to any discussion of switching uses of rooms.

Each of the areas where you might hold the science fair has a number of advantages and disadvantages:

Room	Advantages	Disadvantages
Cafeteria	has tables, but they may not be moveable	set up only after lunchtime
All-Purpose Room	may have tables	rescheduling of other activities; size; may not have tables
Gymnasium	large size	probably will have to cover the floor; no tables
Lobby Area	no rescheduling	irregular size; no tables

Decision 5: Judging?

Many elementary science fairs are organized to encourage participation and to avoid competition. In this case, all projects are given a certificate of participation (an example certificate is given in chapter 10).

Some schools opt for a "real" judging session and will hand out different certificates—or even ribbons or trophies—according to the judges' results. There are benefits (such as recognition for those students who produced the more worthy projects); but, there are obvious drawbacks (hurt feelings; competition between different ages and ability levels; and, of course, the influence of overly helpful parents) that many educators and parents wish to avoid. If you do decide to have an actual judging session, the children will need to make a presentation to the judge or judges. This creates two additional logistical problems: where to find judges and how to arrange for all the children to be present. Judges can be found among the high school and middle school science teachers and from local industries and hospitals. However, the most convenient time for these professionals will be in the evening; and that, of course, will be a difficult time to have all the children to attend.

Fortunately, there is a middle ground, as well. Sometimes high school science majors, high school science fair participants, or high school National Honor Society members can be asked to act as judges for the elementary school science fair. In this instance, these older students are released from their classes for an hour or two to view the children's projects and to provide a noncritical evaluation and suggestion form for each student (an example is provided in chapter 10). The elementary students do not have to be present for this evaluation, but they receive some worthwhile individual feedback for their hard work. Arrangements can usually be made through the high school principal, science department chairperson, or National Honor Society advisor. Often honor societies have a community service requirement for their members that this "judging" will satisfy.

Decision 6: Programs?

No doubt you will plan to have the science fair open to the parents, students, and the general public for at least a limited time—an afternoon or an evening. This can be accomplished simply with no more than a teacher or two and an administrator to serve as hosts; or more elaborately, with programs, signs, announcements, and even refreshments.

If you choose the latter, a little more planning will be required. A program can merely be a list of the students' names or it can also be more elaborate and include the names of the projects, teacher names, a list of judges, the philosophy of your science fair, a list of helpers or parent volunteers, and a cover. Either way will entail someone typing up the information. If you are handy with computers, make a data base very early as soon as you have a list of the participants and add to it as project titles are finalized. You may be able to find a parent volunteer or a secretary who would be willing to help.

Whether the program is alphabetized or listed in order of the project numbers will depend on how much time you have to devote to this part of the planning and organizing. Some science fairs use the "first come, first served" policy of setting up the projects. This is, of course, the easiest method. If you would like to have the projects organized by topics or to display a variety of different subjects in each row or area, then you will need to assign numbers to the students. Index cards on which numbers have been written free-hand can be taped to the tables and a master layout of the table configuration and numbering system can be displayed in several places. Parent volunteers or several of the older children can help with taping the cards on the tables.

CHAPTER 10

Paperwork and Helpful Hints

Some of the problems that arise in organizing a science fair come from weaknesses in communication. The more information everyone has, the smoother the science fair can be conducted. This chapter provides helpful tips for organization, a master checklist for the chief organizer, and the following example forms, letters, and certificates:

- an information letter to parents,
- an information letter to teachers,
- an information letter to judges,
- a student entry form,
- a request for student evaluators,
- an evaluation form,
- a certificate of participation, and
- an announcement.

Since a science fair is a perfect setting for Murphy's Law, the following tips (dealing with supplies, refreshments, judges, illness, weather, workshops, and volunteers) should be considered.

Supplies:

You will probably never have all the supplies you will need for a science fair; so try to keep some funds in reserve for last minute items. Most schools try to supply as many materials as possible for the children, but parents should be aware that they may have to purchase some supplies.

It is helpful to keep a folder with suppliers names and telephone numbers, local businesses that will often help with discounts or donations, and a list of all the items you use. As new materials are needed, add them to the list. By the end of the first year's science fair, you will be in a much better position to anticipate the supplies needed for another year. As a start, try to have on hand the following consumable materials:

- stencils of several sizes
- large and small construction paper
- poster board
- washable markers

The following science supplies that the children may need to borrow should be available if possible:

- balances
- metric rulers
- meter sticks
- Celsius thermometers
- graduated cylinders
- test tubes
- test tube racks
- beakers
- funnels
- filter paper
- cheesecloth
- microscopes
- magnifying glasses
- bar magnets

Additional items that would be very helpful, but may not be available in every school include letter cutters (preferably 2-inch and 3-inch sizes) and large rolls of colored paper. Sometimes churches or clubs have letter cutters that you might be able to borrow.

Be certain to pack extra materials for set-up, because not everyone will remember to bring what they need. The International Science and Engineering Fair, a high school level competition involving students from all over the world, actually contracts with a rental company to provide a huge booth with every imaginable tool, gadget, and supply—from step ladders to electric drills! Your students' needs, of course, will not extend that far; but, you will want to have a good supply of:

- masking tape
- duct tape
- transparent tape
- paper clips
- scissors
- hammer
- pliers
- Philip's screwdriver
- "regular" screwdriver
- markers
- pencils
- tacks
- correction fluid
- blank, stick-on labels

You may want to put a volunteer in charge of this supply box during set-up and have a sign-out sheet to help keep track of the items.

Refreshments:

If you have the science fair open to the public in the evening, simple refreshments can be offered. Often the parents' association will provide punch and cookies. You can also request help from the cafeteria staff or community or school service groups.

Adult judges will appreciate some kind of snack and coffee, tea, and soft drinks. Student judges or evaluators will be pleased with a snack and/or soft drinks. Often you can approach a local grocery store, convenience store, or restaurant for donations.

You may be able to have the student participants donate paper plates, cups and napkins.

Judges:

If you plan to have adult judges, you will need to make arrangements as many months in advance as you possibly can. The easiest pool of judges is high school and middle school science teachers. They will only be available after the school day, in the evening, or on a teacher in-service day (also known as staff development days, teacher days, etc.). It may be difficult to schedule a convenient time, so investigate the teachers' availability before setting the date for your science fair.

Adult judges from local business and industry may be able to accommodate your schedule more easily, especially if you are limited to holding the judging during the school day. Often companies will give professional employees release time for such community service.

You will need to carefully communicate to adult judges about the criteria you wish to have followed for the judging of projects. Sometimes judges will expect too much of elementary school students and sometimes they will expect too little. Also be certain to explain exactly what awards are to be given (every student will receive a certificate, three winners in each field, one overall winner, etc.). You should not need to remind judges that they will want to encourage the child no matter the quality of the project.

Scheduling high school or middle school students for judging or evaluating the projects is generally quite simple, if your science fair will be set up during the day. Contact the principal or science department chair at least a month before your science fair. Depending upon the regulations of your school district and upon the proximity of your school, you may need to provide transportation for middle school students. High school students can usually arrange to drive themselves. A sample letter of request to the principal or science department chair and a sample evaluation form are provided later in this chapter.

Illness:

Be sure to communicate to parents and students your school's policy on student activity participation when a student has been absent from school. Also decide in advance how you will handle the possibility of a child's absence from the judging session and the possibility of a child's extended absence that results in the project not being completed.

Weather:

If you live in an area plagued with snowstorms and if your science fair will be held during that season, it is wise to plan for an alternative date. Make these arrangements known to parents, students, and judges several weeks before the science fair.

The Student's Science Fair Handbook suggests that parents be prepared for rain or winds on set-up day. You will want to remind them to cover the display with plastic (garbage bags will work well) so that it arrives undamaged. It is really sad to see a child's neatly done graphs and lettering smeared by the rain or bent by the wind.

Workshops:

Some schools enlist the help of parents or teacher aides in conducting display workshops for the children during the school day. An unused room or the lobby area can be set up with the letter cutter, poster board, construction paper, markers, and other materials. The students can be excused from class for the morning or afternoon on a rotating schedule to come to the workshop to work on their display.

Workshops for experimentation and consultation can also be offered with the help of middle school, high school teachers, parents, or community members with a science background. These can be held on weekends, after school, or during school. High school students may also be willing to help, but adult supervision would have to be arranged.

Volunteers:

Never underestimate the number of helpers you will need. It is always best to plan for double the number you originally think will be required. Some of the sources of volunteers are parent's associations and community, high school, and middle school service clubs.

You may want to assign volunteers to assist with:
- typing and photocopying forms and letters
- setting up a data base of information
- all aspects of the program
  - typing
  - creating a cover
  - copying
  - stapling
- measuring the rooms that may be considered for the location of the science fair
- finding available tables
- workshops by:
  - arranging for people to help with the workshop
  - locating and organizing the materials
  - providing transportation
  - helping the students
  - helping the teachers
  - escorting the children to and from class
  - storing the work completed
- the set up or removal of projects by:
  - arranging tables and chairs
  - taping numbers on tables
  - serving as guides and hosts

- helping the children with their projects
- providing transportation
- refreshments by:
    - providing some of the snacks or drinks
    - providing paper plates, cups, or napkins
    - setting up the refreshment table
    - serving the refreshments
    - cleaning up
- the judging/evaluating by:
    - finding judges/evaluators
    - helping with refreshments
    - serving as guides or hosts
    - providing transportation
    - helping with the judging or evaluation forms
    - calculating the winners
    - typing or printing student names on the certificates
    - placing certificates on the projects
- publicizing the science fair by:
    - making signs and/or fliers
    - placing signs
    - arranging free advertising on local television and radio
    - placing the information on the school's outside sign
- the public viewing by:

    handing out programs

    serving as hosts

Master Checklist

- ☐ Date:
- ☐ Time for set-up
- ☐ Time for removal
- ☐ Time for Judging/Evaluating
- ☐ Location
- ☐ Snow date
- ☐ Number of students
- ☐ Number of tables
- ☐ Number of judges
  - ☐ List of judges and telephone numbers
- ☐ Number of evaluators
  - ☐ Contact person and telephone number
- ☐ Program
  - ☐ Number needed
- ☐ Certificates
  - ☐ Number needed
- ☐ Awards
  - ☐ Number needed
- ☐ Information letter to parents
- ☐ Information letter to teachers
- ☐ Information letter to judges
- ☐ Student entry forms
- ☐ Judging or evaluation forms
- ☐ Refreshments
- ☐ Workshops
- ☐ Teachers participating
- ☐ Volunteers
- ☐ Publicity
- ☐ Supplies
  - ☐ for workshops
  - ☐ to lend to students
  - ☐ for set-up

Letter to Parents

Dear Parents:

We are having a science fair this year!

All students in _____
are encouraged to participate.

One of the greatest joys of science is discovery. When we give our children a chance to discover something on their own, we provide not only an exciting scientific experience but also a real life experience.

Completing a science fair project allows the child to actually *be* a scientist. While we regularly afford our children an abundance of opportunities to relish the natural world and to sample science, we rarely give them the chance to *experience* science — with its requirements of hard work, tenacity, and creativity.

Our science fair will be held in the _____
_____.

Projects will be set up at _____.

All students will receive a Certificate of Participation.

You will be receiving more detailed information in the near future.

Letter to Teachers

Dear Teachers:

We are having a Science Fair this year!

It will be held on _____ for all students in grades_____.

Please try to incorporate science fair projects into your classroom schedule. There are various time schedules attached that may assist you in coordinating your lesson plans.

The information to be provided to the students and other suggestions and schedules are attached.

Please contact _____ if you have any questions.

We are looking forward to providing a rewarding experience for all.

Letter to Judges

Dear Judges:

Thank you for being willing to help our students with this opportunity to begin to explore scientific experimentation.

We will meet with you in the _____ at _____ School at _____ o'clock for a brief orientation. We will provide judging forms and refreshments.

Our main goals in having you talk with the students individually are to provide them with noncritical feedback about the work that they have accomplished and to give them the opportunity to share their excitement and what they have learned.

We look forward to providing a rewarding experience for all.

Student Entry Form

Parents: Please complete this form with your child and return it to the classroom teacher by _____.

Name of Student _____

Grade _____   Name of Teacher _____

Name of Parent _____

Telephone Number _____

Science Fair Project Topic _____

_____

Signature of Student _____

Signature of Parent _____

Signature of Teacher _____
(Indicates approval of topic)

Letter to High School

Dear _____ :

_____ Elementary School is holding a science fair on

_____ .

    We would like to have some of your students evaluate our projects. They will not be judging them so much as offering encouragement and suggestions for improvement. We will need approximately ___students from one of your service organizations or students who have participated in your science fair.

    Our students will not be present for this evaluation. We have _____ projects and we would like your students to arrive at the _____ at _____ o'clock. It is anticipated that the evaluation process will require approximately ____ hour(s). Evaluation forms will be provided along with some light refreshments.

    If you have further questions, please contact _____ at _____ .

    Thank you for your willingness to assist us in making this important opportunity possible for our students.

ELEMENTARY SCIENCE FAIR COMMENT SHEET

☐   NICE   DISPLAY

☐   GOOD   IDEA

☐   EXCELLENT   PROCEDURE or METHOD

☐   NEATLY   DONE

☐   NICE   MODEL

☐   EXCELLENT   DATA

☐   VERY   CREATIVE

ADDITIONAL   COMMENTS:

Certificate of Participation

Awarded to

For the completion of your Science Fair Project

Presented by

Publicity Announcement

Please announce the following information about this important local elementary school function:

SCIENCE FAIR

AT _____ ELEMENTARY SCHOOL

OPEN TO THE PUBLIC FROM _____ TO _____

ON _____

THERE WILL BE _____ SCIENCE FAIR PROJECTS BY STUDENTS IN

GRADES _____ THROUGH _____

PLEASE COME AND JOIN THESE YOUNG SCIENTISTS!

For further information contact:

_____ at _____

ANNOTATED BIBLIOGRAPHY

1. Ardley, Neil. *The Science Book of Air*. New York: Gulliver Books, Harcourt Brace Jovanovich, Publishers, 1991.
NOTES: 14 simple activities and demonstrations with air.
Several can be made into science fair projects, particularly lung capacity, air trapped in fabric, parachutes, airplane wings, and paper airplanes.

2. ———. *The Science Book of Color*. New York: Gulliver Books, Harcourt Brace Jovanovich, Publishers, 1992.
NOTES: 12 simple activities and demonstrations with color.
Several are suitable for science fair projects. The activities with simple chromatography and sunsets are very good.

3. ———. *The Science Book of Electricity*. New York: Gulliver Books, Harcourt Brace Jovanovich, Publishers, 1992.
NOTES: 13 simple activities and demonstrations with electricity.
There are not adequate safety precautions and many of the activities will require close adult supervision.
Several can be adapted into science fair projects.

4. ———. *The Science Book of Light*. New York: Gulliver Books, Harcourt Brace Jovanovich, Publishers, 1992.
NOTES: 10 simple activities and demonstrations with light.
Several are suitable for science fair projects. The activities with plants and kaleidoscopes are particularly good.

5. ———. *The Science Book of Sound*. New York: Gulliver Books, Harcourt Brace Jovanovich, Publishers, 1991.
NOTES: 14 simple activities and demonstrations with sound.
Several can be adapted into science fair projects, particularly the simple telephone, musical instruments, and reflected sound.

6. ———. *The Science Book of Water*. New York: Gulliver Books, Harcourt Brace Jovanovich, Publishers, 1991.
NOTES: 14 activities and demonstrations with water.
Few are suitable for science fair projects.

7. Asimov, Isaac. *A Stargazer's Guide*. Milwaukee, WI: Gareth Stevens Publishing, 1995.
NOTES: Reference for astronomy-related science fair projects.

Photographs or drawings of the phases of the moon,
constellations, telescopes.
FEATURES: Table of Contents
More Books about Astronomy
Videos
Places to Visit
Places to Write
Glossary

8. ———. *Projects in Astronomy.* Milwaukee, WI: Gareth Stevens Pub., 1990.
NOTES: 13 astronomy activities.
Most do not require a telescope.
Only the activities on sun spots and sundials are suitable for
science fair projects.
FEATURES: Table of Contents
Glossary
Index

9. Blune, Stephen C. *Science Fair Handbook: A resource for teachers, principals,
and science fair coordinators.* Columbus, OH: Merrill Publishing Company,
1989.
NOTES: Useful for planning and setting up a science fair.
Some ideas for science fair projects.
FEATURES: Table of Contents
Reproducible masters for letters, forms, certificates

10. Brin, Susannah, and Nancy Sundquist. *50 Experiments I Can Do.* Los Angeles,
CA: Price Stern Sloan, Inc., 1988.
NOTES: Interesting simple experiments and demonstrations.
Some can be made into science fair projects, particularly fake
fossils, spider webs, bark rubbings, and ants.
FEATURES: Index

11. Burgess, Jeremy. *The Magnified World.* Just look at.... Vero Beach, FL: Rourke
Enterprises, 1987.
NOTES: Fascinating examples of microphotography.
Explains all kinds of microscopes.
Reference for microscope-related science fair projects.
FEATURES: Table of Contents
Books and Places
People
Glossary (Word List)
Index

12. Cassidy, John. *Explorabook: A Kids' Science Museum in a Book*. Palo Alto, CA: Klutz Press, 1991.

> NOTES: A fascinating collection of information and 50+ activities in many fields of science.
>
> A real interest-booster for grades 4 and 5; but only a few, such as the experiments with magnets, can be adapted for science fair projects.
>
> Some safety concerns with the bacteria activities.
>
> FEATURES: Interesting extras are included in the book: a Moiré spinner, agar, Fresnel lens, diffraction grating, mirror
>
> Table of Contents
>
> Riddles and Puzzles

13. Catherall, Ed. *Exploring Light*. Exploring science. Austin, TX: Steck-Vaughn Co., 1989.

> NOTES: 16 simple activities with light.
>
> Actually at a lower level than what is stated (for grades 4-9).
>
> Some can be made into science fair projects.
>
> FEATURES: Table of Contents
>
> Test Yourself
>
> Glossary
>
> Books to Read
>
> Index

14. Catherall, Ed. *Exploring Magnets*. Exploring science. Austin, TX: Steck-Vaughn Co., 1989.

> NOTES: 20 simple activities with magnetism.
>
> There are not adequate safety precautions prescribed and some of the activities will require close adult supervision.
>
> Some can be adapted for science fair projects.
>
> FEATURES: Table of Contents
>
> Test Yourself
>
> Glossary
>
> Books to Read
>
> Index

15. ———. *Exploring Sound*. Exploring science. Austin, TX: Steck-Vaughn Co., 1989.

> NOTES: 18 simple activities with sound.
>
> Some can be made into science fair projects. The activities with sound-proofing, amplification, and musical instruments are very good.
>
> FEATURES: Table of Contents

Test Yourself
Glossary
Books to Read
Index

16. ———. *Exploring Uses of Energy*. Exploring science. Austin, TX: Steck-Vaughn
    Co., 1991.
        NOTES: 20 simple activities with energy.
            Several can be expanded for use as a science fair project,
                particularly pulse rate and simple machines.
        FEATURES: Table of Contents
            Test Yourself
            Glossary
            Books to Read
            Index

17. Challoner, Jack. *The Science Book of Numbers*. New York: Gulliver Books,
    Harcourt Brace Jovanovich, Publishers, 1992.
        NOTES: 11 simple activities and demonstrations with numbers and
            counting.
            Several are suitable for science fair projects, particularly the
                abacus, random numbers, musical instruments, spring
                scale, pulse rate, and sun dial.

18. Cobb, Vicki. *Chemically Active!* New York: J. B. Lippincott, 1985.
        NOTES: Forty-seven experiments in chemistry.
            Safety precautions not adequate.
            Some items/chemicals are now hard or impossible to buy.
            Many can be adapted into science fair projects.
        FEATURES: Table of Contents
            Index

19. Conaway, Judith. *More Science Secrets*. Mahwah, NJ: Troll Associates, 1987.
        NOTES: Good background for scientific principles.
            Some experiments can be developed into science fair projects,
                particularly speed of falling objects, evaporation, friction,
                parachutes, weather station, static electricity, solar energy.
        FEATURES: Table of Contents
            Index

20. Cox, Shirley. *Chemistry*. Vero Beach, FL: Rourke Publications, 1992.
        NOTES: Lists the steps and ideas for doing a project.
            No actual projects are developed.

No instructions for projects are provided.
FEATURES: Table of Contents
List of Suppliers
Glossary
Index

21. ———. *Earth SciencE*. Vero Beach, FL: Rourke Publications, 1992.
NOTES: Lists the steps and ideas for doing a project.
No actual projects are developed.
No instructions for projects are provided.
FEATURES: Table of Contents
List of Suppliers
Glossary
Index

22. Darling, David J. *Making Light Work: the science of optics*. Experiment!
Toronto: Macmillan Publishing Company, 1991.
NOTES: 14 simple and more complex activities with light.
Some can be used as science fair projects. The activities with
color and eye sensitivity, light ray patterns, and the beam
tank are particularly good.
Also explains the scientific principles related to light and
optics.
FEATURES: Table of Contents
Taking It Further
Experiments in Depth
Glossary
Index

23. ———. *Sounds Interesting: the science of acoustics*. Experiment! Toronto:
Macmillan Publishing Company, 1991.
NOTES: 16 simple and more complex activities with sound and
acoustics.
Some can be used as science fair projects. The experiments
with noise and concentration, the speed of sound, and
recording animal sounds are especially interesting.
Also explains the scientific principles related to sound and
acoustics.
FEATURES: Table of Contents
Taking It Further
Experiments in Depth
Glossary
Index

24. Davies, Kay, and Wendy Oldfield. *Electricity and Magnetism*. Starting Science.
          Austin, TX: Steck-Vaughn Company, 1992.
                    NOTES: 10 simple activities with electricity, circuits, and magnetism.
                          Safety is stressed.
                          Only a few of the experiments can be expanded for use as a
                          science fair project.
                    FEATURES: Table of Contents
                          Glossary
                          Finding Out More
                          Index

25. Dixon, Malcolm. *Flight*. Technology Projects. New York: The Bookwright Press,
          1991.
                    NOTES: 18 activities that explain all types of flight technology.
                          Several can be developed into science fair projects, especially
                          parachutes and kites.
                    FEATURES: Table of Contents
                          Glossary
                          Books to Read
                          Places to Visit
                          Index

26. ———. *Land Transportation*. Technology Projects. New York: The Bookwright
          Press, 1991.
                    NOTES: 18 activities that illustrate various forms of transportation.
                          Several can be expanded into science fair projects, especially
                          powered vehicles, streamlining, and roads.
                          Safety is not stressed adequately.
                    FEATURES: Table of Contents
                          Glossary
                          Books to Read
                          Organizations to Contact
                          Places to Visit
                          Index

27. ———. *Structures*. Technology Projects. New York: The Bookwright Press, 1991.
                    NOTES: 15 activities that explain all kinds of man-made structures,
                          such as dams and tunnels.
                          Many can be adapted into science fair projects, especially
                          concrete beam, towers, wood structures, tunnel shapes,
                          and bridges.
                    FEATURES: Table of Contents
                          Glossary

Books to Read
Places to Visit
Index

28. Fredericks, Anthony D., and Isaac Asimov. *The Complete Science Fair Handbook: for teachers and parents of students in grades 4-8*. Glenview, IL: GoodYear Books, 1990.

      NOTES: Useful for organizing a science fair (judging criteria, etc.).
          Much of the information is too advanced for grades 2-5.
          Numerous ideas for science fair projects, but many are not the data-gathering type.
          No example projects nor experimental procedures are provided.
      FEATURES: Table of Contents
          Sample Forms (not for reproduction)
          Resources
          Books for Students, Teachers, and Parents
          Periodicals for Students, Teachers, and Parents
          Government Agencies
          Organizations

29. Gardner, Robert. *Science Experiments*. New York: Franklin Watts. 1988.

      NOTES: Fifty-four interesting activities and projects in various fields.
          Most do not have detailed instructions.
          Most require adult supervision and/or participation.
          Safety precautions are not adequately addressed.
      FEATURES: Table of Contents
          Books for Further Reading
          Index

30. Hamilton-MacLaren, Alistair. *Water Transportation*. Technology Projects. New York: The Bookwright Press, 1992.

      NOTES: 15 activities that explain all kinds of water transportation.
          Some can be adapted into science fair projects, especially floating, detergent-powered boats, candle-powered boats, and airboats.
      FEATURES: Table of Contents
          Glossary
          Books to Read
          Organizations to Contact
          Places to Visit
          Equipment
          Index

31. Hershey, David R. *Plant Biology Science Projects*. New York: John Wiley & Sons, 1995.
    NOTES: 21 experiments with plants.
    Listed for "ages 12 and up," but some are at a level useful for students in 4th or 5th grade.
    More adult supervision will be required.
    Safety precautions are minimal.
    Some can be developed into science fair projects: bean seed imbibition, stomate density, soil pH, fertilizers, mineral deficiencies, and several on seed germination.
    FEATURES: Table of Contents
    Index

32. Jaffe, Roberta and Gary Appel. *The Growing Classroom: garden-based science*. New York: Addison-Wesley Pub. Co., 1990.
    NOTES: 158 activities centered around gardening.
    Useful to build problem-solving skills.
    Some can be adapted into science fair projects, especially those on growth requirements and soil erosion.

33. Katz, Phyllis, and Janet Frekko. *Great Science Fair Projects*. New York: Franklin Watts, 1992.
    NOTES: 24 simple projects with adequate directions.
    Most are consumer-type projects and surveys.
    The experiments suggested with cut flowers, raisins, and birds are good.
    Some safety concerns with mold experiments.
    FEATURES: Table of Contents
    For Further Reading
    Index

34. Kenda, Margaret, and Phyllis S. Williams. *Science Wizardry for Kids*. Hauppauge, NY: Barrons Educational Series, Inc., 1992.
    NOTES: 200+ activities in all areas of science.
    Only a few can be developed into science fair projects, eg. pinhole camera, old-fashioned paint, and bubbles.
    FEATURES: Table of Contents

35. Kramer, Alan. *How to Make a Chemical Volcano and Other Mysterious Experiments*. New York: Franklin Watts, 1989.
    NOTES: Interesting story-like format of 29 simple experiments to do with common household chemicals.

Written by a 13-year-old.

Many can be developed into science fair projects, particularly crystals, chromatography, acid/base indicators, and rusting.

Adequate safety precautions.

FEATURES: Table of Contents

Setting Up a Lab

List of Supplies and Where to Find Them

Index

36. Lambert, Mark, and Alistair Hamilton-MacLaren. *Machines*. Technology Projects. New York: The Bookwright Press, 1991.

NOTES: 15 projects to build that explain many classes of machines.

Most can be developed into science fair projects, especially water clock, windmill, signal light, generator, sorter, screw pump.

Several projects — micrometer, data sorter, and robot arm — can be used as parts of projects on other topics.

FEATURES: Table of Contents

Glossary

Equipment

Books to Read

Useful Addresses

Index

37. Lammert, John. *Human Body*. Science Fair: How to do a successful project. Vero Beach, FL: Rourke Publications, Inc., 1992.

NOTES: Lists the steps and ideas for doing a project

No actual projects are developed.

No instructions for projects are provided.

FEATURES: Table of Contents

List of Suppliers

Glossary

Index

38. ———. *Plants*. Science Fair: How to do a successful project. Vero Beach, FL: Rourke Publications, Inc., 1992.

NOTES: Lists the steps and ideas for doing a project.

No actual projects are developed.

No instructions for projects are provided.

FEATURES: Table of Contents

List of Suppliers

Glossary

Index

39. Markle, Sandra. *Science Mini-Mysteries*. New York: Atheneum, 1988.
    NOTES: 29 demonstration activities of scientific prrinciples.
          Only one, the acid/base activity, can be developed into a
          science fair project. The remainder are simply
          demonstrations that can build interest.
    FEATURES: Table of Contents
          Designing a Science Experiment
          Index

40. ———. *The Young Scientist's Guide to Successful Science Projects*. New York:
    Lothrop, Lee & Shepard Books, 1990.
    NOTES: Gives the steps needed for a project.
          Advanced for this age group, but could be used for 5th grade.
          Offers some ideas of how to find a project idea.
          Safety is not adequately addressed.
    FEATURES: Table of Contents
          Index

41. Martin, Paul D. *Science: it's changing your world*. Books for world explorers.
    Washington, DC: The National Geographic Society, 1985.
    NOTES: Useful background information on technology.
          A bit dated.
          No activities, demonstrations, or projects.
    FEATURES: Table of Contents
          Index

42. McGrath, Susan. *Fun with Physics*. Books for world explorers. Washington,
    DC: The National Geographic Society, 1986.
    NOTES: Useful for explanations of physical phenomena.
          Simple activities to demonstate physical principles.
          Few can be extended into science fair projects.
    FEATURES: Table of Contents
          Index
          Glossary

43. O'Reilly, Susie. *Textiles*. Technology Projects. New York: The Bookwright Press,
    1991.
    NOTES: 17 activities that highlight all kinds of fabrics and their
          properties.
          Many can be adapted into science fair projects, especially
          testing fabrics, making felt, patterns, and dyeing.

FEATURES: Table of Contents
Glossary
Books to Read
Further Information
Organizations to Contact
Index

44. Orii, Eiji, and Masako Orii. *Simple Science Experiments with Light*. Simple Science Experiments. Milwaukee, WI: Gareth Stevens Children's Books, 1989.
NOTES: 6 simple demonstrations of the properties of light.
Useful as an introduction to light.
Several can be developed into science fair projects, particularly shadows and refraction.
FEATURES: Glossary (terms are defined and used in sentences)
Index

45. ———. *Simple Science Experiments with Marbles*. Simple Science Experiments. Milwaukee, WI: Gareth Stevens Children's Books, 1989.
NOTES: 4 simple demonstrations of the momentum.
Only the activity on conservation of momentum can be modified for science fair project.
FEATURES: Glossary (terms are defined and used in sentences)
Index

46. ———. *Simple Science Experiments with Ping Pong Balls*. Simple Science Experiments. Milwaukee, WI: Gareth Stevens Children's Books, 1989.
NOTES: 11 simple experiments with air pressure.
Useful as an introduction to Bernoulli's principle.
None can be used for science fair projects.
FEATURES: Glossary (terms are defined and used in sentences)
Index

47. ———. *Simple Science Experiments with Starting and Stopping*. Simple Science Experiments. Milwaukee, WI: Gareth Stevens Children's Books, 1989.
NOTES: 10 simple demonstrations of inertia.
None can be developed into science fair projects.
FEATURES: Glossary (terms are defined and used in sentences)
Index

48. ———. *Simple Science Experiments with Water*. Simple Science Experiments. Milwaukee, WI: Gareth Stevens Children's Books, 1989.
NOTES: 6 simple experiments with density and displacement.
Only the activity with the density of various liquids is suitable

for a science fair project.
FEATURES: Glossary (terms are defined and used in sentences)
                    Index

49. Oxlade, Chris, and Corinne Stockley. *The World of the Microscope*. London:
     Usborne Publishing Ltd., 1989.
             NOTES: Very good for an introduction to microscope use.
                    Explains how a light microscope and an electron microscope
                          work and applications to the modern world.
                    Contains a large number of interesting activities with
                          microscopes and magnifying glasses. Many are good
                          starter ideas for science fair projects, but all will need
                          thought to develop an intriguing purpose.
                    Many of the diagrams are not drawn to scale and children may
                          become frustated at not finding what the book shows.
                    Safety is not adequately addressed with regard to stains, blood,
                          bacteria, and fungi.
          FEATURES: Table of Contents
                    Equipment
                    Glossary
                    Index

50. Pilger, Mary Anne. *Science Experiments Index for Young People*. 2d Edition.
     Englewood, CO: Libraries Unlimited, Inc., 1996.
             NOTES: A useful index to elementary science activities and
                          experiments in nearly 1500 books.
                    Books listed are both new and old (some are out of print)
                    Also available in a software version.
          FEATURES: Alphabetical Index of Topics from "abacus" to "zoo
                          animals"
                    Index of Books listed alphabetically by author name.
                    Cross-referenced (eg., "baking soda" has an alternative
                          subject of "acids and bases")

51. Prochnow, Dave, and Kathy Prochnow. *How?: more experiments for the young
     scientist*. Blue Ridge Summit, PA: Tab Books, 1993.
             NOTES: Suitable for grade 5.
                    43 demonstrations of how things work (eg., airplanes,
                          helicopters, remote controls) and what causes natural
                          phenomena (eg., winds, comets).
                    Many can be adapted for use as science fair projects.
                    Some require a considerable amount of equipment.
          FEATURES: Table of Contents

Suppliers
Software
Glossary
Index

52. Reed, Catherine. *Environment*. Science Fair: How to do a successful project.
    Vero Beach, FL: Rourke Publications, Inc., 1992.
    NOTES: Lists the steps and ideas for doing a project.
    No actual projects are developed.
    No instructions for projects are provided.
    FEATURES: Table of Contents
    List of Suppliers
    Glossary
    Index

53. Sharman, Lydia. *The Amazing Book of Shapes*. New York: Dorling Kindersley,
    1994.
    NOTES: Many activities with symmetry, patterns, and designs.
    The introduction to tangrams, tessellations, and fractals can be
    developed into science fair projects.
    FEATURES: Table of Contents
    mirror bookmark
    shape stencils
    Glossary

54. Spurgeon, Richard. *Ecology*. Usborne science and experiments. London:
    Usborne Publishing Ltd, 1988.
    NOTES: 34 activities illustrating the study of ecology.
    Only a few, such as soil experiments and making recycled
    paper, are suitable for science fair projects.
    FEATURES: Table of Contents
    Going Further
    Organizations
    Glossary
    Index

55. Symes, R. F., and R. R. Harding. *Crystal and Gem*. Eyewitness books. New York:
    Alfred A. Knopf, 1991.
    NOTES: Very useful for identifying crystals and gemstones (excellent
    color photographs).
    Interesting and broad background information.
    FEATURES: Table of Contents
    Index

56. VanCleave, Janice Pratt. *Janice VanCleave's Machines*. New York: John Wiley & Sons, Inc., 1993.
    NOTES: 20 experiments with simple machines.
       Each type has one "cookbook" experiment followed by suggestions for further experimentation.
       Some can be adapted for science fair projects.
    FEATURES: Table of Contents
       Let's Explore
       Glossary
       Index

57. ———. *Janice VanCleave's Microscopes and Magnifying Lenses: Mind-boggling Chemistry and Biology Experiments You Can Turn into Science Fair Projects*. New York: John Wiley & Sons, Inc., 1993.
    NOTES: 20 activities that introduce the properties of lenses and an appendix with basic information on the use of a microscpe.
       Each activity is "cookbook" style with some suggestions for expansion.
       Some can be developed into science fair projects.
       There are not sufficient safety precautions given for work with bacteria and mold.
       The pond water organisms shown in Appendix 3 are not drawn to scale and are not easily found in most pond water.
    FEATURES: Table of Contents
       Appendices: The Compound Microscope
            Preparing a Wet Mount
            Common Pond Water Organisms
       Glossary
       Index

58. ———. *Janice VanCleave's Rocks and Minerals: Mind-boggling Experiments You Can Turn into Science Fair Projects*. New York: John Wiley & Sons, Inc., 1996.
    NOTES: 20 activities with rocks and minerals.
       Each activity is "cookbook" style with some suggestions for expansion.
       Some (hardness, specific gravity, carbonates, and stalagmites) can be developed into science fair projects by 4th and 5th grade students.
    FEATURES: Table of Contents
       Books

Catalog of Suppliers
Other Sources of Rocks and Minerals
Glossary
Index

59. Walpole, Brenda. *175 Science Experiments to Amuse and Amaze your Friends: Experiments! Tricks! Things to Make!* New York: Random House, 1988.
    NOTES: Simple activities and demonstrations of air pressure, optical illusions, solar energy, etc.
    Only a few, such as the water clock and natural dyes, can be developed into science fair projects.
    FEATURES: Table of Contents
    Quizzes to Check Knowledge
    Glossary
    Index

60. ———. *Counting.* Measure up with science. Milwaukee, WI: Gareth Stevens Publishing, 1995.
    NOTES: Useful as an introduction to graphing and ratios.
    FEATURES: Table of Contents
    Important Events
    For More Information:
        More Things to Do
        More Books to Read
        Videotapes
        Places to Visit
    Index

61. ———. *Distance.* Measure up with science. Milwaukee, WI: Gareth Stevens Publishing, 1995.
    NOTES: Very useful as an introduction to measuring systems and how to measure for science fair projects.
    Includes estimation, triangulation, metric system units, and scale drawing.
    FEATURES: Table of Contents
    Important Events
    For More Information:
        More Things to Do
        More Books to Read
        Videotapes
        Places to Visit
    Index

62. ———. *Size*. Measure up with science. Milwaukee, WI: Gareth Stevens
Publishing, 1995.
        NOTES: Very useful as an introduction to methods for measuring area,
            volume, capacity, weight, and mass for science fair
            projects.
        FEATURES: Table of Contents
            Important Events
            For More Information:
                More Things to Do
                More Books to Read
                Videotapes
                Places to Visit
            Index

63. ———. *Temperature*. Measure up with science. Milwaukee, WI: Gareth Stevens
Publishing, 1995.
        NOTES: Useful as an introduction to temperature.
            9 simple activities with measuring temperature.
            Some can be expanded into science fair projects, particularly
            temperature and growth, insulation, and thermal
            expansion.
        FEATURES: Table of Contents
            Important Events
            For More Information:
                More Things to Do
                More Books to Read
                Videotapes
                Places to Visit
            Index

64. Webster, David. *Winter*. Exploring Nature Around the Year. Englewood Cliffs,
NJ: Julian Messner, 1989.
        NOTES: Activities and things to make and do in the winter.
            A few can be modified into science fair projects.
        FEATURES: Table of Contents
            Index

65. Wong, Ovid K. *Is Science Magic?* Chicago: Childrens Press, 1989.
        NOTES: Interesting, but very few of the 44 demonstrations of natural
            phenomena and scientific principles can be developed
            into science fair projects.
        FEATURES: Table of Contents
            Index

66. Wyatt, Valerie. *Weather Watch*. New York: Addison-Wesley Publishing Company, Inc., 1990.

NOTES: Some simple activities and a great deal of interesting weather information, facts, and quizzes.

None are suitable for science fair projects.

FEATURES: Table of Contents

Index

Appendix A
TIME SCHEDULES

6-Week Schedule

Week 1
Step 1: A Science Fair Project
Step 2: Thinking about a Project
Step 3: Picking a Project
Worksheet 1

Week 2
Step 4: Planning Your Project
Worksheet 2
Step 5: Safety
Step 6: Planning to Gather Your Data
Worksheet 3
Step 7: Getting Ready
Worksheet 4

Week 3
Step 8: Your Experimental Notebook
Step 9: Experimenting (begin and continue through Week 5)

Week 4
Step 10: Writing the Report (begin)
Step 11: The Experimental Method

Week 5
Step 12: Understanding Your Data
Worksheet 5
Step 13: Making Graphs
Step 15: Your Display (begin)

Week 6
Step 14: Your Conclusion
Worksheet 6
Step 10: Writing the Report (finish)
Step 15: Your Display (finish)
Step 16: The Science Fair

8-Week Schedule

Week 1
Step 1: A Science Fair Project
Step 2: Thinking about a Project
Step 3: Picking a Project
        Worksheet 1

Week 2
Step 4: Planning Your Project
        Worksheet 2
Step 5: Safety
Step 6: Planning to Gather Your Data
        Worksheet 3

Week 3
Step 7: Getting Ready
        Worksheet 4
Step 8: Your Experimental Notebook

Week 4
Step 9: Experimenting (begin and continue
        through Week 7)

Week 6
Step 10: Writing the Report (begin)
Step 11: The Experimental Method
Step 15: Your Display (begin)

Week 7
Step 12: Understanding Your Data
        Worksheet 5
Step 13: Making Graphs
Step 14: Your Conclusion
        Worksheet 6
Step 10: Writing the Report (finish)

Week 8
Step 15: Your Display (finish)
Step 16: The Science Fair

10-Week Schedule:

Week 1
Step 1: A Science Fair Project
Step 2: Thinking about a Project
Step 3: Picking a Project
Worksheet 1

Week 2
Step 4: Planning Your Project
Worksheet 2
Step 5: Safety

Week 3
Step 6: Planning to Gather Your Data
Worksheet 3
Step 7: Getting Ready
Worksheet 4

Week 4
Step 8: Your Experimental Notebook
Step 9: Experimenting (begin and continue
through Week 8)

Week 5 through Week 7
Step 10: Writing the Report (begin)
Step 11: The Experimental Method

Week 8
Step 15: Your Display (begin)

Week 9
Step 12: Understanding Your Data
Worksheet 5
Step 13: Making Graphs
Step 14: Your Conclusion
Worksheet 6
Step 10: Writing the Report (finish)

Week 10
Step 15: Your Display (finish)
Step 16: The Science Fair

Appendix A
12-Week Schedule:

Week 1
Step 1:   A Science Fair Project
Step 2:   Thinking about a Project
Step 3:   Picking a Project
          Worksheet 1

Week 2
Step 4:   Planning Your Project
          Worksheet 2
Step 5:   Safety

Week 3
Step 6:   Planning to Gather Your Data
          Worksheet 3
Step 7:   Getting Ready
          Worksheet 4

Week 4
Step 8:   Your Experimental Notebook
Step 9:   Experimenting (begin and continue
          through Week 8)

Week 5 through Week 8
Step 10:   Writing the Report (begin)
Step 11:   The Experimental Method

Week 9
Step 15:   Your Display (begin)

Week 10
Step 12:   Understanding Your Data
          Worksheet 5
Step 13:   Making Graphs

Week 11
Step 14:   Your Conclusion
          Worksheet 6
Step 10:   Writing the Report (finish)

Week 12
Step 15:   Your Display (finish)
Step 16:   The Science Fair

Appendix B

EQUIPMENT AND MATERIALS SUPPLIERS

AIMS Education Foundation
P.O. Box 8120
Fresno, CA 93747
1-209-255-4094
(general supplies, kits, K-6)

Beckley-Cardy
1 East First Street
Duluth, MN 55802
1-800-446-1477
(general supplies, K-6, kits)

Beeler Box Company
125 Sutton Road
Abbottstown, PA 17301
1-800-864-2607
(cardboard science project boards)

Carolina Biological Supply Co.
2700 York Rd.
Burlington, NC 27215
1-800-334-5551
(scientific equipment, biological
supplies, live specimens)

Connecticut Valley Biological
    Supply Co., Inc.
82 Valley Rd.
P.O. Box 326
Southampton, MA 01073
1-800-628-7748
(scientific equipment, earth
science supplies; K-6)

Delta Education
P.O. Box 3000
Nashua, NH 03061
1-800-282-9560
(scientific equipment, biological
supplies, kits; K-6)

Edmund Scientific Co.
101 E. Gloucester Pike
Barrington, N.J. 08007
1-609-573-6250
(scientific equipment; K-6)

Educational Products, Inc.
2516 Fairway Park Drive
Houston, TX 77092
1-800-365-5345
(science fair supplies, books,
display boards, certificates)

ETA
620 Lakeview Parkway
Vernon Hills, IL 60061
1-800-445-5985
(general supplies, kits, K-6 science
catalog)

Fisher Scientific-EMD
485 S. Frontage Rd.
Burr Ridge, IL 60521
1-800-955-1177
scientific equipment, biological
supplies, live specimens, kits; K-6)

Frey Scientific Co.
905 Hickory Lane
Mansfield, OH 44905
1-800-225-3739
(scientific equipment; separate
Elementary Specialties catalog)

Nasco
P.O. Box 901
Fort Atkinson, WI 53538
1-800-558-9595
scientific equipment, biological
supplies, live specimens, kits;
K-6)

Science Kit & Boreal Laboratories
777 East Park Drive
Tonawanda, NY 14150
1-800-828-7777

(scientific equipment, biological
supplies, live specimens)

Showboard, Inc.
P.O. Box 10656
Tampa, FL 33678
1-800-323-9189
(science fair supplies, display
boards, titles: K-6)

Ward's Natural Science
    Establishment, Inc.
P.O. Box 92912
Rochester, NY 14692
1-800-962-2660
(scientific equipment; biological
supplies; live specimens, kits;
K-6)

Index

About the Author

Patricia Hachten Wee (M.S.Ed., Temple University) has taught biology, scientific research, ecology, environmental science, and physical science. She has advised and encouraged students in science fair project work for many years and is the author of *Managing Successful Science Fair Projects* (J. Weston Walch, 1996). Her high school students are regularly finalists in the International Science and Engineering Fair, the Junior Science and Humanities Symposium, and other national science competitions.

In addition to teaching and writing, Mrs. Wee is a freelance copy editor of scientific journals and a planning commissioner for her township.

She and her husband reside in Lancaster County, Pennsylvania, and have five grown children and two grandchildren.